MW00772276

RIGHT-BRAIN
LEARNING
IN 30 DAYS

THE 30-DAY HIGHER CONSCIOUSNESS SERIES

Right-Brain Learning in 30 Days is the fifth of an ongoing St. Martin's Press New Age 30-Day series. Also available are *Enhanced Memory in 30 Days: The Total-Recall Program; Inner Sex in 30 Days: The Erotic Fulfillment Program; Mystical Experiences in 30 Days: The Higher Consciousness Program; Have an Out-of-Body Experience in 30 Days: The Free Flight Program;* and *Lucid Dreams in 30 Days: The Creative Sleep Program.* All of these titles are written by Keith Harary, Ph.D., and Pamela Weintraub, and can be either specially ordered through your bookstore if currently not in stock, or directly ordered through St. Martin's Press by writing: St. Martin's Press, Customer Service, 175 Fifth Avenue, New York, NY 10010.

New titles to complement this New Age series will be released in the coming months and subsequent years.

We would like to hear about your experiences with the Whole Mind Program for possible inclusion in a new book. Please contact us at:

The Institute for Advanced Psychology
Box 875
2269 Chestnut Street
San Francisco, CA 94123

RIGHT-BRAIN LEARNING IN 30 DAYS

THE WHOLE MIND PROGRAM

KEITH HARARY, PH.D., AND PAMELA WEINTRAUB

ST. MARTIN'S PRESS NEW YORK

For organic chemistry, a pain in the left brain,
and a pleasure in the right.
—Pamela Weintraub

For Anne Goldberg, whose dedication to teaching inspired
generations of students to learn and to write.
—Keith Harary

RIGHT-BRAIN LEARNING IN 30 DAYS: THE WHOLE MIND PROGRAM. Copyright © 1991 by Keith Harary, Ph.D., and Pamela Weintraub. All rights reserved. Printed in the United States of America. No part of this book may be used or reproduced in any manner whatsoever without written permission except in the case of brief quotations embodied in critical articles or reviews. For information, address St. Martin's Press, 175 Fifth Avenue, New York, N.Y. 10010.

Library of Congress Cataloging-in-Publication Data

Harary, Keith.
    Right-brain learning in 30 days / Keith Harary and Pamela
Weintraub.
        p.   cm.   —(Higher consciousness 30-day series)
    ISBN 0-312-06452-7 (pbk.)
    1. Imagery (Psychology).   2. Visualization.   3. Dreams.
4. Cerebral dominance.   5. Self-actualization (Psychology).
I. Weintraub, Pamela.   II. Title.   III. Series.
BF367.H35   1991
153.3—dc20   91-21806
                                                                        CIP

First Edition: September 1991
10 9 8 7 6 5 4 3 2 1

CONTENTS

INTRODUCTION

A good friend of ours, now a successful professional, almost failed to graduate from high school because of his seeming inability to grasp the basics of a required course in accounting. He found the teacher's approach to the subject so tedious, in fact, that he ultimately stopped attending class. On the morning of the final exam he was truly in a precarious position.

In the last hour before the exam, our friend inwardly confronted accounting for the first time. Sitting alone in the schoolyard, he tried to make some sense out of the course textbook. Since there was no time to read the book from cover to cover, however, he studied the various diagrams and ledgers and virtually ignored the printed text. Soon his conscious awareness of his body and the surrounding environment seemed to fade. He began feeling aroused and focused at a deep inner level, as though nothing else existed but the pictures of the various accounting forms depicted in the book.

With a flash of insight he recognized that the forms followed a predictable pattern—a holistic, three-dimensional pattern that seemed to come alive in his mind. He suddenly felt as if he were part of another reality, a reality consisting entirely of numbers and ledgers. He found himself imagining all sorts of complicated accounting problems in his head and mentally picturing the way they would be expressed and handled on paper. But the paper he imagined wasn't lying flat in a notebook or on a desk. It seemed to surround him like an animated hologram that was visible from every direction. Emerging from that intense mental experience, the student managed to maintain his sense of inner focus. He took the test and achieved an almost perfect score. His only mistake was a single misplaced decimal point, which was only a typographical error!

As unusual as this story may sound, we have heard similar reports from many others studying and working in a wide variety of fields. Their experiences confirm what many educators and psychologists now contend: that there are optimal states of mind that are especially conducive to accelerated learning. These mental states have, in recent years, been associated with the right brain. By turning down the engine of the left brain (associated with rote learning and analysis) and revving up the right brain (associated with intuition, visualization, and spontaneity) students can get to the *aha!* phase of learning. They can grasp skills or subjects in a new, profound, and potentially deeper way.

Scientists have long known that the human cortex—the part of the brain responsible for self-awareness and higher cognitive functions such as language and abstract reasoning—is divided into left and right hemispheres. They have spent more than a hundred years studying these hemispheres, using accident and stroke victims in which a known section of the brain has been impaired. As early as 1836 a French doctor found that damage to the left hemisphere impaired his patients' ability to speak, while damage to the right hemisphere did not. Subsequent studies revealed that the left hemisphere controls the right part of the body and perceives the right visual field, while the right hemisphere controls the left part of the body and perceives the left visual field.

This basic knowledge paved the way for the classic "split-brain" experiments, orchestrated by Nobel Prize–winning California Instituate of Technology psychobiologist Roger Sperry in the Fifties. Sperry's experiments relied on a neurological structure called the corpus callosum—an isthmus of nerve cells that connects the right hemisphere to the left. Working with patients whose callosal fibers had been severed to control epilepsy, Sperry revealed whole new facets of the brain. Allowed to see a picture with only the left-brain visual field, for instance, a split-brain patient could verbally identify the image as a flower, say, or a house. But if the patient saw the same image with only the right-brain visual field, he would be unable to speak about it at all. That same patient, on the other hand, could visually identify and then point to a similar image of the flower or the house. Just because the right brain was "mute," Sperry's research showed, it really wasn't less conscious than the left brain—it just had a different point of view.

In years of follow-up research with split-brain patients, accident victims, and people who had half of their brains anesthetized, Sperry and a host of other neuroscientists attempted to further delineate the specialized functions of the right and left cerebral hemispheres. The left hemisphere, they determined, was involved in those tasks that required analytical reasoning and linear logic. The right brain, on the other hand, seemed to be involved in visual tasks such as recognizing faces, spatially manipulating objects, and organizing and synthesizing disparate bits of information such as reading or interpreting maps. While the left brain could memorize material and learn by rote or plod through reams of text analytically to find an answer, the right brain could say *aha!*—it could have direct, immediate, emotional, and seemingly in-tuitive responses to data, perceiving the underlying patterns in a flash.

Most of this experimental evidence has been gathered from right-handed people, which leaves open the question of whether the roles of the right and left hemispheres may be reversed in those who are left-handed. In fact, until scientists study both right- and left-handed people, as well as other groups, it will be impossible to definitively map the anatomical sites of various brain functions. But while the different cognitive modalities are not necessarily limited to the right and left hemispheres, we will, for the sake of clarity, use the terms right brain and left brain throughout this text.

Among the first to marshal the powers of the right brain for learning were sports scientists, who taught athletes to achieve intensely focused "flow" states so they could immerse themselves more deeply in their athletic performances. Back in the Seventies, for example, Colorado State University researcher Richard M. Suinn was called upon to help his school's Alpine ski team. To test his technique, Suinn divided the team into two groups. The first group skied as it always had. But the second group was helped to enter an altered state of consciousness known as alert relaxation, in which the mind remains acutely alert while the body is deeply relaxed. After the test group of skiers had relaxed, they practiced a visualization technique called "controlled dreaming," in which the deep imagination and concentration associated with a dream combines with the conscious awareness and self-control associated with a waking state. In that paradoxical state of consciousness, Suinn's skiers were asked to envision themselves practicing their athletic skills: skiing slalom courses, racing downhill, and finishing a race.

"The method worked so well," Suinn recalls, "that the study itself almost flopped." During practice sessions, the trained skiers performed so much better than those in the control group that the coach never really gave the control group skiers a chance to compete. Nonetheless, as a result of this success, Suinn's method—which he calls visuo-motor behavior rehearsal—found its way to Olympic athletes competing in the Nordic skiing, biathlon, and pentathlon events.

For these athletes, tapping into the visual and experiential mode of thought enhanced their learning power and subsequent success. But as many educators and psychologists have found in recent years, the powers of the right brain are not only useful to those who wish to study a sport. No matter if your subject is art, auto mechanics, organic chemistry, or French, opening up nonlinear and nonverbal channels of thought can help you learn in a new, more expansive, and frequently more rapid way.

Opening up these right-brain channels is our goal in *Right-Brain Learning in 30 Days: The Whole Mind Program*. In fact, as you experience the exercises that follow, you should find yourself becoming more adept at absorbing new concepts and mastering complex skills that may have bogged you down before.

You'll start, in Week One, by quieting your left brain so that the powers of your right brain can come to the fore. You will, for example, create a special study space and collect a small library of music conducive to right-brain learning. You will also learn to enter the altered state of alert relaxation and hone your visualization skills. Finally, during Week One, you will begin to focus on vital right-brain territory—the realm of dreams.

In Week Two you will focus on intensifying the right-brain skills developed during Week One. You will further hone your powers of visualization through a series of guided imagery exercises, for example, and learn to use humor as a means of stimulating the unconscious. You will also journey further into the realm of dreams. You will learn about dream incubation, an ancient technique that allows you to deliberately influence the subject matter of your dreams. You will also learn how to induce lucid dreams, in which you are aware that you are dreaming while the dream is in progress. By doing so you will begin directing the hidden potential of your right brain toward your subject in an ever more powerful way.

In Week Three, you will begin to integrate your newly acquired right-brain learning skills with the left-brain learning techniques you have no doubt used in the past. After all, just because right-brain learning is effective, it doesn't mean you should abandon tried and true—and, certainly, essential—techniques such as reading the textbook or developing a fuller understanding of your chosen topic in a logical, sequential, step-by-step way. To help you utilize right-brain and left-brain techniques in concert, you will learn to read and write—distinctly left-brain activities—with a right-brain spin. You will seek out metaphors in written and moving images, and also pursue a more active, real-world involvement with the topic at hand.

Finally, in Week Four you will attempt to reach the zenith of right-brain learning—the Zen state—in which you become totally immersed, on the deepest level possible, in the subject you wish to learn. During Week Four, you will learn how to empty your mind of all distractions and to stay in what psychologists call *the zone*—that intensely focused realm where your brain works in perfect harmony with your topic and everything simply clicks.

Before you get started on the Whole Mind Program, we'd like to suggest that you choose a topic you especially wish to study. While our program is meant to teach the techniques of right-brain learning for a wide range of subjects, focusing on one topic for the 30-day period should make it easier for you to master the right-brain techniques. For optimum results, you might choose a field of study about which you currently know little but would like to know much more in the next 30 days. (Of course, if you are currently immersed in a topic, you can follow through with that subject instead.)

We also want to remind you that although the Whole Mind Program has been created around a 30-day format, you may feel free to modify it to fit your schedule and needs. Indeed, every person is unique and each topic brings to the right-brain learning arena different constraints and needs. In the end, you will custom-design your own program based on the Whole Mind exercises you have practiced over the course of weeks.

Above all, right-brain learning should take you closer to the subject you want to learn. Our exercises cannot make you an expert in 30 days, of course, but they should help to accelerate and deepen your learning process during this period. They should also make it easier to learn about things that have stumped—and maybe even stopped—you in the past. Perhaps most important, as you continue to practice the Whole Mind exercises, you should reap the joy of intellectual and intuitive intimacy—even unity—with your chosen field.

WEEK ONE

TURNING ON THE RIGHT BRAIN

WEEK ONE

•

TURNING ON THE RIGHT BRAIN

*I*n Week One of the Whole Mind Program, you'll begin practicing the core techniques that can help you turn on your right brain. Most psychologists and educators working with right-brain learning have found that one of the major impediments to full functioning of the right brain is the left brain itself. The pragmatic, common sense, chatty left brain is so often dominant in helping us negotiate the everyday world, it seems, that signals from the right brain sometimes have trouble getting through to conscious awareness.

The techniques presented in Week One will help you turn down the volume of the voluble left hemisphere, making room for a view from the right. To start the process, you will first learn to practice the technique of alert relaxation, in essence entering an altered state of consciousness in which your mind remains completely alert while the muscles of your body become deeply relaxed. You will also get into the habit of playing baroque music, which moves to the rhythm of sixty to seventy beats a minute, much like the resting human heart. Tapping these methods and others, you will gradually slow the chatter of the left brain, so that your right brain can emerge.

Once you have turned on your right brain, Week One exercises will help you explore this rich, uncharted realm. In one technique, for instance, you will enlist all your senses as you explore a chosen terrain. As you apply the lessons of this multisensory practice session to your chosen field, be it African American history or deep-sea diving, you should begin to perceive the broader global patterns involved.

Finally, Week One will introduce you to what Sigmund Freud called "the royal road to the unconscious"—the realm of dreams. As you begin to recall and explore the content of your dreams, you will establish closer, more frequent contact with the intuitive, creative part of your mind and open additional pathways for communication with your right brain.

As you begin the Whole Mind Program and experiment with our right-brain techniques, remember that more traditional left-brain learning strategies are also useful and effective and should not be abandoned. To be sure, you probably have developed your own preferred learning strategies, based on a lifetime of learning experiences, that have worked well for you in the past. To create a balanced and effective approach to learning, you should continue to use those existing successful strategies while tapping the right-brain techniques as well.

DAY 1

CREATING A RIGHT-BRAIN REFUGE

No matter what task you wish to master or the nature of the subject you wish to learn, your ability to focus will be greatly enhanced if you take the time to create a special learning environment. On Day 1, therefore, you'll focus on creating a right-brain refuge.

There's a good reason for setting aside a particular day for organizing and equipping your right-brain learning environment: The simple act of choosing a suitable location in which to study should stimulate your right brain (and your deeper unconscious mind), preparing it to absorb entirely new information. As you prepare this room, you should feel much like a child entering the first grade with a boxful of freshly sharpened pencils and a brand new notebook: Just having those symbolic and essential items on hand told the deepest part of you that something different and special was about to happen.

Begin by choosing a location—preferably one in or near your home—that is quiet and peaceful, conducive to such internal activities as fantasy and visualization. Indeed, whether your chosen subject is essentially intellectual (organic chemistry, for example) or physical (tennis or golf), your refuge should enable you to focus without interruption.

Whenever possible, your right-brain refuge should be particularly geared to the subject you plan to study. For instance, if you want to become a gourmet cook, you might create a right-brain refuge in your kitchen. If you are learning to speak Hebrew, on the other hand, your refuge might be in your bedroom or a private office in your home. If you are learning a sport like judo, your right-brain refuge might be set up as a properly equipped workout room or gym. If you are learning auto mechanics, your right-brain refuge will no doubt be set up in your driveway or garage. If you are learning to drive a car, your right-brain refuge might be the car itself.

Make sure these special places are properly equipped. If you are learning to play billiards, your right-brain refuge might include such items as a pool table, cues, chalk, bridge, rack, and balls. If you are learning auto mechanics, you'll need a complete and well-organized set of tools, along with all the appropriate parts and fluids for each particular learning session. If you chosen subject requires an office environment, you should equip the space with comfortable furniture, as well as all the books, office supplies, and office equipment you'll be needing in the coming weeks. If you are learning some athletic skill, you should take this time to gather the proper equipment and clothing, as well as such basic niceties as fresh soap and clean towels.

To the greatest extent possible, your right-brain refuge should be a place in which you feel supremely comfortable on both an emotional and physical level. For instance, there may be several potential office sites within your home, or more than one area in which to work out or tinker around. Choose a spot where you feel you will learn best.

Perhaps most important, make sure to equip your refuge with the special tools of right-brain learning: You should have easy access to a tape recorder to help you through guided imagery exercises and provide you with music. (A second audio source, such as a stereo, CD player, or tape deck, would be helpful as well.) Make sure that your refuge is equipped with a comfortable couch or chair for visualization, guided imagery, and focusing activities; paper for right-brain drawing and writing; and adequate ventilation.

—If you are setting out to master a subject or activity that simply cannot be simulated in the immediate vicinity of your home—skiing, say, or driving—we suggest that you create a right-brain refuge that will at least enable you to visualize the chosen activity. While it's true that the ski slopes may be hundreds of miles from your home, you will still be able to use your right-brain refuge to do a large number of the creative visualization and fantasy exercises so crucial for right-brain learning. You may also use your car as a right-brain refuge as long as you leave it parked while using it in this capacity.

Once you have taken these basic steps toward creating your personal right-brain refuge, you should go a step further and fill your special space with appropriate stimuli for all your senses. If you are studying an African language, for example, take some time to supply your right-brain refuge with African pictures and objects, African music, even the sounds of African wildlife and the tastes of African food. You might equip your refuge with native African clothing or jewelry, which you can wear when studying or doing right-brain exercises. (You may wear these right-brain props throughout the day as well.) These props will surely provide you with an enhanced sense of connectedness to the culture behind the language you are learning. Remember, by deliberately immersing yourself in your subject matter on as many sensory levels as possible, you'll be making yourself especially receptive to absorbing new information on a right-brain level.

DAY 2

UNDER THE VOLCANO

Most of us find ourselves tensing up when preparing to enter into a new learning task. Much of this tension originates with the fear of failure and the belief that learning anything is an inherently difficult process. Psychologists and educators have found, however, that a relaxed, confident, and open-minded frame of reference is much more conducive to learning. Perhaps more important, a state of deep relaxation will help you gain access to your right brain. As the active volcano of complete waking consciousness gives way to a calmer, more centered state of mind, the multisensory impressions and associative connections of the right hemisphere will be freer to emerge.

To help you reach this goal, Day 2 will focus on achieving the state of alert relaxation, in which your body becomes deeply relaxed while your mind remains acutely alert. To enter this special state, you will first create a guided imagery tape, in which a series of words and images help to guide you under the volcano of your mind. As you enter the state of alert relaxation, your conscious mind should begin to com-municate more easily with your innermost self. Right-brain and left-brain learning skills will then have the chance to more effectively interact, and a powerful intellectual synthesis should result.

Before you begin this exercise, you'll need a couple of basic tools: a cassette recorder and a blank tape. Once you have these essentials, label the tape ''Under the Volcano'' and retire to your right-brain refuge. Then, when you have at least half an hour of peace and quiet, record the following words on the tape. Make sure to speak slowly and carefully, pausing where indicated.

> **Hemispheric Hint**—If you have a friend with a particularly clear or mellifluous voice, you may want to have him or her read the section instead. It is sometimes easier to enter the state of alert relaxation to the sound of a voice other than your own. In any event, after a week or so you may decide that you don't need the help of this guided imagery tape in order to enter the state of alert relaxation. Instead, you should be able to go under the volcano simply by going through the images in your mind.

Begin your recording with the words below:

> Take a deep breath, let it out slowly, stretch your muscles, and relax. Now imagine that warm currents of mental energy are very slowly moving up through the soles of your feet toward your ankles.
>
> Feel the muscles in your feet gradually warming and relaxing as you imagine the currents passing through them. [Pause.] Imagine that the currents continue moving up through your calves [pause], into your thighs [pause], through your hips [pause] and buttocks [pause], and into your lower back and abdomen. [Pause.] Proceed very slowly, giving yourself time for each group of muscles to begin fully relaxing before allowing the imaginary currents to move on to the next area of your body. [Pause.] Feel the muscles in your legs becoming heavy, warm, and relaxed and sinking down into the chair beneath you. [Pause.]
>
> When you feel your legs becoming deeply relaxed, imagine the currents moving in a clockwise motion around your abdomen [pause], then up along your spine [pause], and through the front of your torso into your chest [pause] and shoulders. Feel the muscles in your stomach and lower back letting go of any tightness or tension as the current passes through them. Allow a feeling of general well-being to begin flowing through your body with the imaginary currents as you feel your body relaxing. [Pause.]
>
> When the lower half of your body feels relaxed [pause], imagine the currents flowing upward through your ribs and shoulders [pause], warm-

ing and relaxing the upper part of your body [pause], and leaving your back and chest feeling completely warm and free of any stress or tension [pause]. Imagine the currents turning around to move downward through your arms, toward your fingertips [pause], swirling around through your fingers and hands, then moving upward once more and back through your arms and neck toward the top of your head. [Pause.]

Now feel the muscles in your neck and face gradually becoming warm and relaxed as the imaginary currents pass through them. [Pause.] Then imagine the currents flowing out through the top of your head [pause], leaving your entire body feeling comfortably warm [pause], heavy [pause], and relaxed [pause], and sinking down into the chair beneath you.

After you or a friend has created an "Under the Volcano" tape, you may begin the exercise itself. To do so, enter your right-brain refuge and make sure the light is at a comfortable level—not glaring, but bright enough to allow you to read and write. Sit down in a comfortable chair, stretch your muscles, relax, and take a deep breath. Then turn on the tape recorder and close your eyes.

After the recording has finished, turn the tape recorder off (or allow it to switch off automatically) and focus on maintaining the desired state. Remember, do not allow yourself to become so deeply relaxed that you'll find it hard to concentrate. Rather, focus on gently calming yourself and getting into a receptive state of mind for absorbing new ideas while still remaining fully aware of your surroundings. Should you find yourself accidentally falling asleep while practicing this exercise, however, don't worry about it. The moment you wake up and realize what has happened just continue carrying out the exercise, without moving, from wherever you left off. At this point you'll probably already be quite relaxed, so the key will be to become even more deeply relaxed without once again falling asleep.

In order to maintain the desired state of alertness, you may find it helpful to imagine the warm currents passing through your body in a variety of changing colors and patterns. You may also find it helpful to practice this exercise only when you are feeling physically and emotionally rested and easily able to remain awake.

Hemispheric Hint—As you progress through the Whole Mind Program, you'll be incorporating many other exercises and techniques into your alert relaxation sessions. On Day 3, for instance, you'll follow your "Under the Volcano" tape with baroque music, which is said to enhance the alert relaxation experience and, according to some studies, the ability to absorb new information. On Day 2, however, you will focus only on maintaining the state of alert relaxation without trying to do anything else. This core technique will aid you in the days and weeks of right-brain learning to come.

Once you have achieved a deeply relaxed, mentally alert state, you should maintain it for anywhere from fifteen minutes to half an hour. At that point, you can begin to bring yourself out of the state of alert relaxation and back to ordinary waking consciousness. To do so, wiggle your fingers and toes, slowly stretch your muscles, open your eyes, and sit up.

DAY 3

BASTION OF THE BAROQUE

Back in the Sixties, Bulgarian psychiatrist Georgi Lozanov reported that when his students listened to baroque music, they increased their ability to absorb and recall information. The reason, Lozanov believed, was related to the tempo of the music. At sixty to seventy beats per minute, the rate of baroque music is similar to that of the resting human heart. As a result, say Lozanov and many of his colleagues, the music induces an altered state of consciousness—a state particularly conducive to learning. More recently, this notion has been supported by other researchers studying brain waves. Baroque music, these scientists have shown, stimulates alpha waves, the brain waves associated with alert relaxation and a sense of calm. Since alert relaxation is so conducive to learning, on Day 3 you will add baroque music to the "Under the Volcano" tape you made on Day 2. In addition, you will collect other baroque tapes, CDs, or LPs so that you have a repertoire of baroque music to play as you participate in the various right-brain exercises and as you proceed to learn.

To begin, get a recording of at least two hours of baroque music. Some of the best baroque composers include Bach, Boccherini, Corelli, Fasch, Handel, Haydn, Mozart, Schubert, and Vivaldi. We particularly recommend Schubert's "Trout" Quintet in A Major for Piano and Strings, Vivaldi's Guitar Concerto in D Largo, Vivaldi's Flute Concerto in D, Mozart's Piano Concerto no. 21, and Handel's Harp Concerto in B-flat. Of course, you may have some other favorite baroque compositions, and you may use those instead.

After you have your baroque music library at hand, we suggest you pick twenty minutes of your favorite piece and record it at the end of your "Under the Volcano" tape. Then, whenever you have a bit of extra time, you can use this element to deepen your alert relaxation state.

After you have made these preparations, enter your right-brain refuge. As before, make sure the light is at a comfortable level—not glaring, but bright enough to allow you to read and write. Sit down in a comfortable chair, stretch your muscles, relax, and take a deep breath. Then turn on the tape recorder and close your eyes. As you play the "Under the Volcano" tape with the added section of baroque music, once more enter a state of alert relaxation.

After the recording has finished, turn the tape recorder off and focus on maintaining the desired state. Remember, do not allow yourself to become so deeply relaxed that you'll find it hard to concentrate. Rather, focus on gently calming yourself and getting into a receptive state of mind for absorbing new ideas while still remaining aware of your surroundings.

In order to maintain the desired state of alertness, you may find it helpful to imagine the warm currents passing through your body in a variety of changing colors and patterns. When the music section begins, you may also envision the musical notes and melodies as a cascade of colors.

Once you have achieved a deeply relaxed, mentally alert state, you should attempt to maintain it for a full thirty minutes (including the period of time during which the baroque selection plays).

After half an hour has passed, you can begin to bring yourself out of the state of alert relaxation and back to full waking consciousness. To do so, wiggle your fingers and toes, slowly stretch your muscles, open your eyes, and sit up.

Hemispheric Hint—Your "Under the Volcano" tape with baroque music should serve as a wonderful prelude to any study or work session, no matter what the topic. For the next four weeks, and whenever you need a boost in "getting into your subject" in the months and years ahead, feel free to play this tape before your work session begins.

DAY 4

RIGHT-BRAIN
DRAWING

The right brain is inherently visual. To help you tune into your right brain, therefore, we present a drawing exercise adapted from a technique created by California State University art professor Betty Edwards, author of the excellent book *Drawing on the Right Side of the Brain*. Not only will the exercise below demonstrate the awesome power, insight, and interpretive skill of the right brain, it will also provide you with another pathway into that realm of your mind.

Before you begin, find a picture you would like to draw. You may choose the picture from an art or photography book, from a magazine or newspaper, from a text book, or from your personal mementos. If possible, choose a picture related to the topic you wish to study. Also gather two sharpened, number-two pencils and a few sheets of 8½-by 11 white paper. Take these supplies and retire to your right-brain refuge. (If you don't have a desk or writing surface in your right-brain refuge, make sure you get a large, hard-backed book to lean on while drawing.)

Hemispheric Hint—Since drawing is such a nonverbal task, we suggest that you read the rest of the instructions through before continuing the rest of the exercise.

To begin, play your "Under the Volcano" tape, complete with the selection of baroque music you added on Day 3. When you have finished listening to the tape, you should be in the state of alert relaxation. Now take your chosen picture and turn it upside-down. Then, paper and pencil in hand, begin to copy the picture. Start your drawing at the top and work your way down. Do not try to recognize or give names to any objects, individuals, or specific aspects of the picture. Instead, just pay attention to the lines and angles, the areas of shadow and areas of light.

After you have finished the drawing, turn it right-side-up. You may be amazed to see that you have captured the picture with more accuracy and detail than you ever could have had you copied it from the upright position. If you never thought you had artistic talent, this little experiment might cause you to change your mind.

The reason this technique is often so successful is that the act of drawing upside-down suppresses the left brain and helps the right brain come to the fore. The upside-down images, says Edwards, cause recognition problems for the analytic left brain. The visual right brain, on the other hand, easily grasps the relationship between lines, angles, and shapes.

In short, this little exercise has helped you prime your right brain —it has helped you make a cognitive shift so that your right brain holds sway.

Now that you've made this shift, we'd like you to spend some time engaged in learning your chosen topic. If you're studying French cooking, whip up a soufflé. If you're studying organic chemistry, look at the chemical structures of the organic molecules and try to get a visual feel for their three-dimensional shapes. If you're studying the Civil War, envision what it would have been like to be in the midst of the struggle. See yourself as a Union soldier, for instance, and picture the gruesome details of the battle of Gettysburg in your mind's eye.

After you've spent at least an hour immersed in your chosen field, take another piece of paper and draw a second picture. This time draw an image taken from your mental impression of the learning experience of the last hour. After you have drawn the picture, take a few moments to look at it and then, without verbalizing what it tells you, simply put it aside.

DAY 5

MULTISENSORY MIND

During Day 3 you learned to tap your right-brain capabilities more effectively through music. During Day 4 you tuned into your right brain by focusing on your sense of vision. On Day 5 you will stimulate your right-brain potential through the nonvisual and nonauditory senses, including touch, motion, taste, and smell. As you begin to absorb information through these alternative senses, often relegated to the sidelines in the learning process, you should develop a clearer internal map of whatever it is you want to learn. In fact, as far as we are concerned, multisensory learning can enhance absorption of virtually any subject.

To explain the value of this technique, we like to quote the innovative educator Linda Verlee Williams from her fascinating book *Teaching for the Two-Sided Mind*. "Let's take a simplified look at what happens when a child handles a cube," Williams says. "As her fingers move over the cube's surface, sensory receptors in the skin of her fingers and hands (the tactile system) send messages to the brain with information about how the cube feels; at the same time, receptors in her muscles and joints (the proprioceptive-kinesthetic system) send information on the movement of her fingers and hands. In the brain, sensations from the touch and movement systems are integrated to give a 'picture' of the object. If the child is looking at the cube, the visual system also supplies information to the brain, and signals from all three systems create an image of the object. Through this experience, the child builds up a concept of the cube and its attributes; she moves from sensory experience to concept formation."

As Williams puts it, "the learner is like a television set that can receive information on several channels." As learners, we usually rely on our visual or auditory senses. But by including your other, often neglected, senses in the learning process, you can grasp ideas, concepts, and techniques in a more holistic, more innate, more *right-brain* way.

There's another advantage to multisensory learning: Opening up the spectrum of sensory channels helps you to shift your point of view and enables you to view the world in surprising ways. These altered and expanded perceptions should, of course, strongly enhance creativity. And the more creative you are—the more open you are to associative, free-flowing thoughts—the more right-brain learning you will be able to achieve.

To help you open all your sensory channels while learning, we present another core Whole Mind technique, below. To begin today's exercise, ask a friend to fill your right-brain refuge with a series of objects rich in texture and form. These may include clothes, figurines, dishes, or toys—virtually anything you have not carried into the refuge yourself. Your friend might also bring items with assorted scents—special soaps and perfumes, freshly cleaned laundry, or powdered cinnamon—as well as foods with distinct or unusual tastes. Once your friend has left your right-brain refuge, turn the lights down low, close your eyes, and play your "Under the Volcano" tape followed by twenty minutes of baroque music. As the music plays, think of the special subject you have chosen to learn.

Then, after twenty minutes, your eyes still closed, shut off the music and explore your right-brain refuge with your nonvisual, nonauditory senses. Before setting out, dim or even turn off the lights in your right-brain refuge, since you should have little or no visual stimulation during this part of the exercise. Also make sure that your surroundings are quiet, and that external sounds do not filter in. If it's impossible for you to shut out the sounds of the outside world, you may wear earplugs or headphones, or get a radio and tune it so that all you hear is static, otherwise known as "white noise."

Then set out to explore. Feel your way past the walls, immerse yourself in the texture of fabrics and take special note of the novel objects contributed by your friend. Taste the food you have been brought and discern its nature from the taste alone. Smell the various objects in your right-brain refuge, and sense the way smells change as you move from one object and one section of the room to the next. Rely on your sense of touch, taste, and smell to create an internal, right-brain map of the room.

Hemispheric Hint—You should, of course, take all due precautions and remove potentially dangerous items.

After you've explored your right-brain refuge environment in this fashion, stop, stand still, and, with your eyes still closed, pay attention to your breathing. Inhale, and feel your breath moving down deep inside of you. Exhale, and feel the breath moving back out of your body into the surrounding air. Inhale, and feel the oxygen once more moving into your lungs, into your bloodstream, and then into every cell of your body. Exhale, and feel carbon dioxide moving out of your body into the atmosphere around you.

Now focus on the beating of your heart. Feel your heart reverberating within your body, pushing blood throughout your chest and stomach, arms and legs. Keep your eyes closed and focus on your heartbeat for a minute or two.

Now focus on the blood moving through your veins. Feel your blood moving through the natural conduits of your body from your chest through your arms to the tips of your fingers, and then from your chest through your legs to the tips of your toes. Feel your blood traveling up into your brain, enriching all the cells of your thinking organ with oxygen and nutrients. Feel the cells of your brain perking up and sharpening their reflexes for the task of learning ahead.

Now focus your sensory awareness back out of your body toward the external world. (Remember, your eyes should still be closed.) As you do so, notice how your nonvisual, nonauditory senses overlap, complementing each other and responding all at once. As you continue to explore your right-brain refuge, think of your sense of smell, touch, motion, and taste as unique powers that help you probe and communicate

with selected aspects of your environment on a special level. Notice
how your sense of yourself and reality slightly shifts its dimensions
each time you focus your attention on a different sense or combination
of senses.

Finally, take a deep breath, open your eyes, and notice the ways in
which your awareness of yourself and your environment subtly shifts
in that moment. Take a few minutes to adjust to your overall experience
and to visually observe the immediate area around you.

Concentrate, while looking around without otherwise moving, on
the full range of visual information that floods your senses in the moment
that you open your eyes. Notice how your sudden focus on your sense
of vision changes the way you relate to and interpret the input of all
your other senses. Concentrate on gathering as much visual information
as possible about the right-brain refuge you have just explored with
your other senses. Notice the tiny details and the ways in which these
details combine to form a greater visual whole.

Now sit in the center of your right-brain refuge and take another
deep breath. Notice the way you perceive color, and the way in which
this perception influences your overall sense of reality. Notice the colors
you've chosen to wear for this occasion, then look for various shades
of these colors in your immediate and more distant environment. If
your right-brain refuge includes a window, or if it is outdoors, look
into the distance and notice the way the world around you seems to
narrow and fade into the horizon. A grain of sand in your immediate
area can become more or less personally significant than a mountain in
the distance, depending entirely upon where you focus your visual
attention.

Now leave the silence of your right-brain refuge and enter an outer
room, or even the outside world—anywhere that the normal sounds of
life emerge to surround you. Notice the ways in which your awareness
of yourself and your environment subtly shifts as sounds come back
into play.

Concentrate on the full range of auditory information that floods
your senses the moment you step back out into the world of sound.
Notice how your sudden focus on your sense of hearing changes the
way you relate to and interpret the input of all your other senses.

As you walk through the outside world with the full range of your
senses in play, soak up your perceptions of your environment. Don't
analyze any of these perceptions, but simply allow them to flow through
you. Then pay attention to various combinations of your senses, and
the way these are influenced by your immediate and more distant environment. Focus, for example, on your senses of smell and hearing.

If you are at the beach, listen to the waves crashing on the sand and notice the way you can smell the wetness all around you. Now focus on your vision and sense of taste. Notice the shifting patterns of light in the waves and taste the salt in the air. Now focus on your sense of touch and hearing. Listen to nearby sounds and sounds in the distance, while feeling the clothes you're wearing touching your skin, and the way the ground feels beneath you.

After you've completed this exercise, take a break and spend the rest of the day having fun or carrying out activities that don't involve the Whole Mind Program. This will give your mind a chance to integrate the experiences you've had today without stressing you out.

DAY 6

RAIN FORESTS
FOREVER

On Day 6 of the Whole Mind Program, you'll combine the alert relaxation and baroque music techniques you learned on Days 2 and 3 with another core right-brain learning technique: guided imagery, in which a scripted scenario can help to guide your conceptual right brain through images of anything you might wish to study, from a rain forest to the universe to the carburetor of your car.

In future weeks you'll custom design a guided imagery script to fit your particular topic, but during Day 6 you will focus on a rain forest. This exercise will help you hone your powers of visualization for the weeks of right-brain learning ahead.

If possible, you should practice today's exercise in some comfortable spot in your right-brain refuge, or someplace nearby where you can safely enter a state of alert relaxation without being disturbed or disturbing anyone else around you. (In other words, we don't recommend trying this exercise while you're driving a car or operating a blender!) Before you begin, arrange to play about an hour of baroque music in the background while carrying out the creative visualization portion of this session.

Hemispheric Hint—Because some preparation is required, please read through all the instructions for Day 6 before you begin. Please note, the first part of the guided imagery exercise presented below essentially re-iterates the alert relaxation instructions from the "Under the Volcano" exercise on Day 2. Pause where indicated, as before.

Begin your recording with the words below:

Take a deep breath, let it out slowly, stretch your muscles, and relax. Now imagine that warm currents of mental energy are very slowly moving up through the soles of your feet toward your ankles.

Feel the muscles in your feet gradually warming and relaxing as you imagine the currents passing through them. [Pause.] Imagine that the currents continue moving up through your calves [pause], into your thighs [pause], through your hips [pause] and buttocks [pause], and into your lower back and abdomen. [Pause.] Proceed very slowly, giving yourself time for each group of muscles to begin fully relaxing before allowing the imaginary currents to move on to the next area of your body. [Pause.] Feel the muscles in your legs becoming heavy, warm, and relaxed and sinking down into the chair beneath you. [Pause.]

When you feel your legs becoming deeply relaxed, imagine the currents moving in a clockwise motion around your abdomen [pause], then up along your spine [pause], and through the front of your torso into your chest [pause] and shoulders. Feel the muscles in your stomach and lower back letting go of any tightness or tension as the current passes through them. Allow a feeling of general well-being to begin flowing through your body with the imaginary currents as you feel your body relaxing. [Pause.]

When the lower half of your body feels relaxed [pause], imagine the currents flowing upward through your ribs and shoulders [pause], warming and relaxing the upper part of your body [pause], and leaving your back and chest feeling completely warm and free of any stress or tension [pause]. Imagine the currents turning around to move downward through your arms, toward your fingertips [pause], swirling around through your fingers and hands, then moving upward once more and back through your arms and neck toward the top of your head. [Pause.]

Now feel the muscles in your neck and face gradually becoming warm and relaxed as the imaginary currents pass through them. [Pause.] Then imagine the currents flowing out through the top of your head [pause], leaving your entire body feeling comfortably warm [pause], heavy [pause], and relaxed [pause], and sinking down into the chair beneath you. [Pause.]

As you feel yourself becoming more and more relaxed, imagine that you are entirely surrounded on all sides by a lush and endless rain forest.

[Pause.] Notice the smells of the earth and greenery all around you [Pause.] Notice the perfumed smells of tropical flowers [pause], the smells of animals [pause], and the feeling of the forest wind brushing your face. [Pause.] Notice the sunlight filtering through leaves and branches far above your head. [Pause.] Listen to the sounds of jungle birds calling in the distance and animals climbing through the brush and overhead branches. [Pause.] Take a deep breath and, as you slowly let it out, imagine your awareness expanding to fill the forest all around you. [Long pause.] Now take another deep breath and slowly, gradually, let that breath out. [Pause.] Remain relaxed, calm, and comfortable. Allow a feeling of complete well-being to flow through you. Imagine yourself shrinking down to the size of the tiniest droplet of water sitting on the floor of the forest. Then feel yourself soaking down into the ground [pause] and being sucked up into one of the tangled roots of a powerful tree. [Pause.] Feel yourself passing through the tiny hairs on the end of the root [pause] and into the root itself. [Pause.] Notice how it feels to be inside of the dark, narrow, moist root. [Pause.] Then feel yourself getting sucked up into the main column of the tree itself. [Pause.] Observe the different layers of wood and bark that surround you. Sense the fresh smell of wood and bark, and tune into the moisture of all the other water droplets surrounding you. [Pause.] Notice the diversity of scurrying, voracious insects living in the outer layers of the tree. Watch a lizard running up the outside of the bark. [Pause.] Notice how dark and close it is inside the trunk. [Pause.] Feel yourself being drawn up through the trunk into one of the upper branches. [Pause.] Notice every other branch in the upper part of the tree. Feel yourself being drawn from the branch into one of the leaves. [Pause.] Notice the warmth of the sunlight on your leaf. [Pause.] Notice the fresh, green, leafy smell. [Pause]. Feel an ant walking on your leaf. Feel yourself disseminating as the leaf uses part of your essence to generate food for the tree, so that the tree may generate more leaves and then grow. Feel that part of yourself becoming one with the tree, comprising the fabric—the very heart—of its physical being. [Pause.] Feel the other part of your essence bubbling out through the leaf and dissolving in the air. [Pause.] Feel yourself passing up out of the leaf and into the sky as a vapor. [Pause.] Become part of a passing cloud. [Pause.] Then float over the rain forest, drifting higher and higher and higher until the rain forest itself turns into a green speck on the planet Earth. [Pause.] Go higher still, until the Earth looks like a blue speck floating in space. [Long pause.] Take a deep breath, wiggle your fingers and toes, open your eyes, and allow yourself to drift gradually back into a state of ordinary waking awareness.

After you or a friend has created the "Rain Forests Forever" tape, you may start the guided imagery process at any point. To do so, enter your right-brain refuge and make sure the light is at a comfortable level. Sit down in a comfortable chair, stretch your muscles, relax, and take a deep breath. Then turn on the tape recorder and close your eyes. If possible, your second sound system should be playing baroque music in the background. (If that is not possible, put on a tape of baroque music after the guided imagery tape has come to an end.) Now your mental journey to the inner rain forest can begin.

> **Hemispheric Hint**—After you have completed this guided imagery exercise, finish listening to the baroque recording. Then allow yourself at least twenty minutes to return to full waking awareness before proceeding with any other activities you may have planned for today.

DAY 7

THE REALM OF DREAMS

One of the most familiar and well-traveled routes any of us can follow into the realm of the right brain lies along the path of dreams. You may have noticed, for example, that dreams not only express your deepest thoughts and feelings, but also may reveal spontaneous insights into any problems that concern you. These spontaneous insights emerge because the right brain—the seat of intuition and spontaneity—is hard at work while you dream. In essence, the material absorbed during the day is reprocessed at night in dreams, and a powerful synthesis of the subject occurs. Often, a deeper, more intuitive understanding of your field is the result.

In fact, the creative leaps attributed to synthesis of material during sleep are legion: Robert Louis Stevenson, for instance, says that the plot for *The Strange Case of Dr. Jekyll and Mr. Hyde* first appeared to him in a dream. The German chemist Fredriech August Kekule said that he intuited the elusive shape of the benzene molecule from a dream. And Elias Howe, inventor of the sewing machine, says that his brain-child also came to him in a dream.

Of course, the conceptual power of the sleeping brain would be more useful to most of us if it could be regularly tapped. If we could remember the insights in our dreams, it might be easier for us to carry them into waking consciousness. That's the raison d'être for our final core technique: "Learning in Dreamtime." This simple exercise is nothing more than a means of heightening your waking awareness of your dreams. After all, if your right brain *has* been synthesizing and conceptualizing while you sleep, your learning effort should be enhanced if you simply recognize the process while awake.

> **Hemispheric Hint**—Next week you will take your dream work further with what dream researchers call dream incubation. Dream incubation allows you to consciously influence the subject matter of your dreams by intentionally focusing on certain thoughts and images just prior to falling asleep. By focusing on the topic you are trying to learn, then dreaming about it at night, you may enhance the way in which your unconscious mind processes the material at hand.

> **Hemispheric Hint**—Because some preparation is required, please read through all the instructions for Day 7 before you begin.

A prerequisite for dream learning is remembering, recording, and appreciating your dreams. As the first part of the Day 7 exercise, therefore, we suggest that you begin by setting up a dream diary.

Your personal dream diary should be a notebook that you can store under your pillow or carry around during the day. Thus, we suggest an easy-to-carry spiral memo pad; if you run out of space on this pad, you can easily purchase another that looks essentially the same. While you're selecting a notebook for your dream diary, you should also select a special pen. We suggest an easy-flowing felt-tip pen that will enable you to write while lying down. The pen used for writing in your dream diary should not be used for anything else. You may also find it helpful to attach a penlight to your dream diary, in case you find yourself waking up and remembering a dream in the middle of the night. Take the notebook you've chosen home with you before writing in it, and place it, along with the pen and penlight, under the pillow on your bed. Then say to yourself: *This is where I'll be recording my dreams*. Leave the notebook under your pillow until you're ready to go to bed.

Once you've set up your dream diary, go about the rest of your day. As you travel to work, shop at the supermarket, or take your kids to the park, observe the people around you and repeat these words silently to yourself: *Everybody has dreams.* Consider the meaning of this phrase and try to imagine what the various people around you might have dreamed last night. Glimpsing the current surroundings, ask yourself what they might dream tonight. What might you dream tonight?

Then, quietly say to yourself: *From now on, I'll remember my dreams.* As soon as you acknowledge your willingness to remember your dreams, let go of the whole idea and forget about it for the rest of the day.

Later, after you've gone to bed, reaffirm your willingness to remember your dreams. Once again, let go of this thought the moment that you acknowledge it, and avoid putting any psychological pressure on yourself. Then fall asleep.

To retain your dreams as completely as possible upon waking up tomorrow morning, you must first understand that dream memories can be as fleeting as your next breath of air. Therefore, whenever you start to wake up, be it in the middle of the night or first thing in the morning, do not open your eyes or even move. Instead, take a while to stop and reflect on your past night's dream experiences. It is very important that during your first waking moments you focus entirely on recalling your dreams.

For this reason, it's best to arrange your sleeping environment to avoid even the tiniest distractions. If you usually sleep with or near another person, ask them not to disturb you before you get out of bed in the morning. If you usually wake up with the aid of an alarm clock, we suggest going to sleep early enough the previous evening so that you'll be likely to wake up long before the alarm would normally go off. (If you absolutely can't do without an alarm, set your clock radio to wake you up with soft, classical music.)

As you engage in dream recollection, don't pressure yourself to remember detailed and convoluted dream descriptions in exact chronological order. As you have probably found when trying to recapture other memories—such as the title of some forgotten song from your unconscious mind—dream memories are best approached with subtlety and grace. They must be allowed to steep—to emerge gradually and spontaneously into your conscious waking awareness.

You are most likely to remember details or fragments of your most recent dream upon first awakening. The thoughts, feelings and images pertaining to this dream can often be gently followed in reverse order to gradually guide you back toward subtle recollections of your earlier dream experiences.

Recollections of earlier dreams, however, are typically as fragile as soap bubbles floating on the wind; they consititute the most subtle feelings and images gently blowing through the hidden passages of your unconscious mind. Any sudden movement in your thoughts, any momentary distraction, any attempt to force the memory, can burst the bubbles and cause the images to evaporate before they fully appear in your waking awareness.

Remember, you must relax, and most important, give yourself time to remember your dreams. If dream images don't instantly float to the surface of your conscious awareness, just lie still for a while, your mind a blank, and see what happens.

To keep your dream journal, give each dream a title as you record it. Also make sure that you always record the date and approximate time of your dreams. For each particular day, keep track of which dream you had earlier in the sleep cycle, and which you had later on. As you write, be sure to note the setting or settings in which each dream occurred, the characters who populated the dream, any significant props or symbols that stand out in your mind, and any thoughts and feelings that the dream may have triggered. We also strongly recommend that you use your dream journal to explore the relationship between your daily concerns and activities—especially the subject you are currently involved in learning—and your dreams. Leave one or two blank pages after each dream entry so that you can add any additional thoughts or recollections that may occur to you as time goes on. Finally, when you record the images and symbols that comprise your dreams, make an effort to interpret their special meaning to you. Although it is not mandatory, feel free to draw any pictures that relate to your dreams; visual images can express the underlying meaning of your dreams in graphic form, or even trigger the release of deeper memories.

Hemispheric Hint—Get into the habit of writing down your dream descriptions just after waking up and before getting out of bed. The longer you wait, the more likely it is that these memories will fade or become distorted.

Hemispheric Hint—As you progress through the Whole Mind Program, you must continue to work on your topic in the left-brain mode as well. Remember, the right-brain techniques are meant to complement, not replace, more conventional aspects of learning, including going to classes, studying textbooks, and doing anything else that's required to master the total spectrum of the material at hand.

Congratulations! You've just completed Week One of the Whole Mind Program. We suggest you celebrate by enjoying some of the more mundane aspects of your life—go to the bookstore and buy a thriller, go bowling, or order a pizza and eat it in front of the TV at home.

DAY 1 CREATING A RIGHT-BRAIN REFUGE		**DAY 2** UNDER THE VOLCANO	
Choose a quiet and peaceful location appropriate to your chosen subject and conducive to fantasy and visualization. If you are setting out to master a subject or activity that cannot be simulated in the immediate vicinity of your home, create a right-brain refuge that will at least enable you to visualize the chosen activity. Make sure the location you choose is properly equipped for learning about your subject. Equip your refuge with the special tools of right-brain learning, in-	cluding a tape recorder, a stereo, CD player, or tape deck, a comfortable couch or chair, and paper for right-brain drawing and writing.	Create a guided imagery tape, using the script provided. Label the tape "Under the Volcano." After you have created the tape, enter your right-brain refuge. Sit in a comfortable chair, stretch your muscles, get comfortable, relax, and take a deep breath. Turn on the tape recorder and close your eyes. After the recording has finished, turn the tape recorder off. Focus on gently calming yourself and getting into a receptive state of mind for absorbing new ideas while still re-	maining conscious of your surroundings. Maintain a deeply relaxed, mentally alert state for 15 to 30 minutes. Bring yourself out of the alert relaxation state and back to complete waking consciousness by wiggling your fingers and toes, slowly stretching your muscles and opening your eyes.

DAY 3
BASTION OF
THE BAROQUE

DAY 4
RIGHT-BRAIN
DRAWING

Organize a collection of at least two hours of baroque music.

Pick 20 minutes of your favorite piece and record it at the end of your "Under the Volcano" tape.

Enter your right-brain refuge. Sit in a comfortable chair, stretch your muscles, relax, and take a deep breath. Turn on the tape recorder and close your eyes.

Play the "Under the Volcano" tape with the added section of baroque music and once again enter a state of alert relaxation.

After the recording has finished, turn the tape recorder off. Focus on gently calming yourself and getting into a receptive state of mind for absorbing new ideas while still remaining conscious of your surroundings.

Maintain a deeply relaxed, mentally alert state for a full 30 minutes, including the period of time during which the baroque selection plays.

After half an hour has passed, bring yourself out of the alert-relaxation state and back to complete waking consciousness by wiggling your fingers

and toes, slowly stretching your muscles, and opening your eyes.

Find a picture you would like to draw. If possible, choose a picture related to the topic you wish to study.

Gather two sharpened, number-two lead pencils and a few sheets of 8½-by-11 white paper. Take these supplies and retire to your right-brain refuge. (If you don't have a desk or writing surface in your right-brain refuge, bring along a large, hard-backed book to lean on while drawing.)

Play your "Under the Volcano" tape, complete with the selec-

(continued)

WEEK ONE TURNING ON THE RIGHT BRAIN (continued)

DAY 4 RIGHT-BRAIN DRAWING		DAY 5 MULTISENSORY MIND	
tion of baroque music you added on Day 3. Listen to the tape and enter a state of alert relaxation.	After you have finished the drawing, turn it right side up and reflect upon your work.	Ask a friend to fill your right-brain refuge with a series of objects rich in texture and form.	After 20 minutes, turn off the music. With your eyes still closed, explore your right-brain refuge with your nonvisual, nonauditory senses.
Open your eyes and sit up. Then, take your chosen picture and turn it upside-down.	Spend at least an hour engaged in learning your chosen topic.	Once your friend has left your right-brain refuge, turn the lights down or off. If it's impossible for you to shut out the sounds of the outside world, wear earplugs or tune a radio so that all you hear is static.	Stop, stand still, and, with your eyes still closed, pay attention to your breathing.
Paper and pencil in hand, begin to copy the upside-down picture. Start your drawing at the top and work your way down.	Take another piece of paper and draw an image taken from your mental impressions of the past hour's learning experience. After you have drawn the picture, reflect upon your work without verbalizing what it tells you, then simply put it aside.		Focus on your heartbeat and the blood moving through your veins.
Do not try to recognize or name any objects, individuals, or specific aspects of the picture. Instead, just pay attention to the lines and angles, the areas of shadow and areas of light.		Close your eyes and play your "Under the Volcano" tape followed by 20 minutes of baroque music. As the music plays, think about the special subject you have chosen to learn.	With your eyes still closed, tune your sensory focus back toward the external world. Notice how your nonvisual, nonauditory senses overlap and complement each other.

DAY 6
RAIN
FORESTS
FOREVER

Continue to explore your right-brain refuge. Focus on your sense of smell, touch, motion, and taste as unique powers that help you probe and communicate with selected aspects of your environment.

Notice how your sense of yourself and reality slightly shifts its dimensions each time you focus your attention on a different sense or combination of senses.

Take a deep breath, open your eyes, and notice the ways in which your awareness subtly shifts in that moment.

Leave your right-brain refuge and notice the sounds of life that emerge to surround you.

Pay attention to various combinations of senses, and the way these are influenced by your immediate and more distant environment.

Prepare your Day 6 guided imagery tape.

Choose a comfortable spot in your right-brain refuge or someplace nearby. Make sure the light is at a comfortable level —bright enough to read.

Sit in a comfortable chair, stretch your muscles, get comfortable, relax, and take a deep breath.

Turn on the tape recorder and close your eyes. If possible, your second sound system should be playing baroque music in the background. (If this is not possible, put on a tape of baroque

music after the guided imagery tape has come to an end.)

Enter a state of alert relaxation and follow the guided imagery instructions on the tape.

Return to full waking awareness.

WEEK ONE TURNING ON
THE RIGHT BRAIN (continued)

DAY 7
THE REALM
OF DREAMS

Choose a notebook for your private dream diary, along with a special pen and penlight. Take these three items home with you and place them under the pillow on your bed. Say to yourself: "This is where I'll be recording my dreams."

After you've set up your dream diary, go about the rest of your day. In the course of your day, observe the people around you and repeat these words: "Everybody has dreams." Try to imagine what the people around you might dream.

Vow to remember your dreams.

Arrange your sleeping environment to avoid even the tiniest distractions. Then, once you've gone to bed, reaffirm your willingness to remember your dreams.

Whenever you start to wake up, be it in the middle of the night or first thing in the morning, do not open your eyes or even move. Instead, stop and reflect on your past night's dream experiences.

Record your dreams in your dream journal.

WEEK TWO

MAKE A RIGHT AT MAGIC MOUNTAIN

WEEK TWO

•

MAKE A RIGHT AT MAGIC MOUNTAIN

*I*n his classic novel *The Magic Mountain*, Thomas Mann describes a young man who visits a sanitorium high in the Alps. With its distilled air, mystical ambience, and distance from the workaday world, Mann's mountain retreat altered the young man's perspective so that it would never be the same.

Week Two of the Whole Mind Program will, we hope, help carry right-brain learners to a similar realm. By enhancing the Whole Mind visualization and imagery techniques so that learners go further, deeper, and faster, into the topic of their choice, Week Two should strengthen your overall right-brain learning skills.

In one of the focal points of Week Two, you will learn how to incubate dreams on your topic of choice. As you dream about your chosen subject, the material should penetrate your deepest self, and your right brain should begin to express—and synthesize—the material in new and enlightening ways. In a more advanced version of dream incubation, you will also learn how to incubate *lucid* dreams, in which you recognize the act of dreaming while in the midst of the dream. Whether your topic involves the Great Wall of matter recently discovered by cosmologists or the civilization of ancient Greece, lucid dream incubation can help you invoke those realms and explore them at will.

Week Two exercises will also teach you to enhance your powers of visualization while awake. You will learn to create (and, of course, call upon) an inner mentor who can help you explore your subject. You will learn to create your own visualization and guided imagery exercises, much as a movie director creates a film. And you will even tap the resources of your right brain through humor. Indeed, there is often a kind of humor barrier that must be traversed before learning can become intuitive on every level. As you call up your wackiest sensibilities, right-brain learning will be enhanced.

In short, Week Two exercises aim to help you make right-brain learning a natural part of your life. As you incorporate right-brain skills into your everyday experience, you should be able to use them anywhere. One person we know recently tapped Week Two exercises to study a driving manual while waiting on line for the written part of her driving test. Though she had only an hour to study the complex and unfamiliar material, visualization techniques helped her get a score of 100 on the exam.

DAY 8

LEARNING IN DREAMTIME

Now that you've learned the basics of dream work, you're ready to practice bona fide dream learning through dream incubation. Dream incubation is a technique in which you intentionally induce a dream on a specific subject by focusing on that subject before falling asleep. By deliberately inducing dreams about your chosen subject, you can place it more thoroughly in the context of right-brain synthesis and thought.

Dream incubation may be as complex as spending days in a special environment meditating and practicing elaborate rituals. Or it may be as simple as quietly telling yourself to dream about a certain topic just before falling asleep. The dream-incubation technique we recommend for the Whole Mind Program is simple and effective, and with practice should provide you with increasingly greater influence over the subject matter of your dreams.

The first part of the process involves turning your dream environment into an extension of your right-brain refuge—that is, creating a sleep space in which your right brain feels free to emerge. To achieve the desired effect, you must subtly transform your sleep environment without intruding upon the overall quality of your sleep.

Begin Day 8, therefore, by reflecting on the psychological atmosphere of your usual sleep environment. Consider the possible influence that any objects or images within this setting may have on your dreams. Are your immediate sleep surroundings rich in stimulating and nurturing images, such as works of art and pictures of your loved ones? Or is your bedroom sterile, marked by stark visual images and piles of work you've brought home from the office? Do you sleep and dream in quiet surroundings, or is the atmosphere frequently jarred by sounds of passing traffic or a television playing in another room? Is the usual temperature of your sleep environment comfortable? Is the ventilation adequate? Is the color of your room soothing to your spirit, or do you find it over-stimulating or just plain boring? Most important: What messages do you receive from your sleep environment? What does it say about your personal relationships and values, and what does it reflect about your attitudes toward sleep and dreaming?

Once you have considered the issues above, make your dream room as calm and comfortable as possible. Decorate it with some favorite objects that express the most positive aspects of your personality. Do your best to make the room attractive, and remove any disturbing or intrusive images that might interfere with dream exploration.

After you have taken these preliminary and psychologically healthy steps, take a look around the room and consider some ways in which you may gently introduce certain aspects of your chosen field of study. The idea is to introduce some subtle background stimuli that will nudge you toward a gentle awareness of your chosen subject as you get ready for bed and eventually drift off to sleep. You should, however, resist the desire to turn the entire room into an endless commercial for a particular subject.

You might, for example, place an attractive bowl of fruit on a dresser if you are learning to paint still lifes, or you might place a copy of the *Wall Street Journal* on your night table if you're working toward your M.B.A. You might hang up an attractive picture of a snow-covered mountain if you are learning how to ski, or a couple of nicely framed movie posters if you are studying the history of film. It certainly isn't necessary to go overboard and turn your entire bedroom into a mock-up of a country general store, complete with open pickle barrels and an assortment of farming implements, to encourage yourself to dream about the early settlers of the Old West.

Once you've made your sleep environment conducive to dream incubation, it's time to induce a relevant dream. First, place your dream diary, special pen, and penlight (if you use one) in a prominent spot beside the bed. Then, as you prepare yourself for sleep tonight, focus on your chosen subject, gently excluding all other thoughts from your mind. Calmly tell yourself that you expect to dream about your field tonight, and that you'll remember the dream when you awaken. If you want, you may further enhance the atmosphere by burning incense or playing music particularly conducive to your desired dream.

Then, just before you finally turn off the light for the night and go to sleep, take a few moments to articulate the topic of your prospective dream in a single sentence, such as "I'd like to dream about being with Adolf Hitler in his Berlin bunker," if your chosen field of study is World War II history, or "I'd like to know what it must be like to be a skid row bum," if your chosen field is the sociology of American cities. Then, using your special pen, write the phrase in your dream diary. As soon as you finish doing this, turn off the lights and go to sleep.

Continue focusing on the phrase you've written in your dream diary. Then, as you fall asleep, picture the special objects or pictures you've placed around you in the room. Gently remind yourself to dream about the subject at hand, and to gain insights into your unconscious feelings toward it while you sleep. Remind yourself, also, that you will remember all related dreams when you wake up.

> **Hemispheric Hint**—Keep in mind that you may not necessarily dream about precisely the question you have phrased in your diary, nor do we expect the dream itself to provide you with the kind of essential analytic information normally gleaned from left-brain learning. Indeed, as far as we're concerned, the old myth about being able to absorb a foreign language by listening to a tape recording in your sleep is an entertaining fiction. The point of this exercise—and the entire Whole Mind Program—is not to replace those modes of learning that you have traditionally found successful in your everyday life. Rather, the dream-incubation technique is intended here to help create a conducive underlying frame of mind. Using this technique, you will facilitate your learning experience by becoming more fully absorbed on a deep inner level in the subject matter of your chosen field. By incubating dreams about your field of study, you will give your creative self an opportunity to express its own inner experience of the material at hand. You may also achieve a sense of personal intimacy toward the subject matter that is hard to come by through a strictly left-brain approach.

> **Hemispheric Hint**—When you wake up, remember to practice the dream-recollection techniques you learned on Day 7. Before moving or opening your eyes, concentrate on your most recent dream experience. Follow these thoughts backward toward earlier images and impressions of the night's dreams. Record any dreams in your journal immediately after opening your eyes.

DAY 9

THE INNER
MENTOR

What would it be like to study impressionistic paint-
ing with Vincent Van Gogh, psychoanalysis with Sigmund Freud, or
mystery writing with Sir Arthur Conan Doyle?

On Day 9, you'll explore this question on an imaginary level through
a guided imagery exercise designed to put you in touch with your own
inner mentor. The inner mentor is, quite simply, that part of yourself
most intimate with your own internal learning process. It is the familiar
voice in your head that speaks to you while you read through a text on
your chosen subject, or that whispers in the back of your mind as you
practice some complicated maneuver like landing an airplane on your
first solo flight. In short, your inner mentor is really your own innermost
intuitive self. On Day 9, you'll deliberately imbue a part of your inner
self with the personality of an expert in your chosen subject, creating
a kind of dialogue that should facilitate your overall learning experience.

Hemispheric Hint—Because some preparation is required, please read
through all the instructions for Day 9 before you begin.

Begin, as you did on Day 6, by choosing a comfortable spot where
you can relax in your right-brain refuge. Then play your "Under the
Volcano" tape with the added selection of baroque music. After you
have spent twenty to thirty minutes in a state of alert relaxation, arrange
to have sixty to ninety minutes of baroque music playing in the background. As the music plays, have a friend gently and slowly read you
the "Inner Mentor" guided imagery instructions that follow. If a friend
is unable to participate, make a tape recording of these instructions and
simply play them back after the "Under the Volcano" tape is complete.
The words to "Inner Mentor" follow:

As you feel yourself becoming more and more relaxed, allow your
thoughts to drift to a time and place that you associate with a sense of
inner peace. [Pause.] The spot may be a serene picnic area by the
beach, for example, or a favorite seat at Shea Stadium. [Pause.] It
can also be a place you've never actually been, such as a magnificent
vista in the Northwest Passage or the middle of the Brooklyn Bridge at
sunrise on a Sunday morning. [Pause.] It can even be an imaginary

place, such as the mythical Shangri-La or a 1950s malt shop on Hollywood Boulevard.

The time and place you choose for this portion of the exercise need not have any obvious or direct relationship with your chosen subject. [Pause.] As you continue to relax and envision your chosen location, allow your mental pictures to become as vivid and realistic as possible. [Pause.] Don't just think of the lush greenery of the picnic area, for example, but notice the wind blowing gently through each blade of grass. [Pause.] Don't just picture yourself sitting at Shea Stadium, but notice the paint peeling off of the wooden bleachers. Gradually allow yourself to involve more and more of your senses in the experience—feel the snow of the Himalayas chilling the bottoms of your feet at Shangri-La. [Pause.] Smell the hot dogs at Shea Stadium and listen to the cheering crowd. [Pause.] Notice the sunlight playing off the metal cables of the Brooklyn Bridge and feel the vibrations of cars passing by on the nearby roadway. [Pause.] Taste the rich egg creams at the malt shop and envision aspiring young actors walking in and milling about. [Pause.] Continue to imagine your chosen location for the next ten minutes. [Long pause of 10 minutes here.]

Now imagine what it would be like to have a personal guide or mentor who completely understands not only every aspect of your chosen field, but also your own innermost thoughts and feelings. [Pause.] Imagine, in as much detail as possible, exactly what this individual looks like. Would he or she be an Olympic athlete, a famous scientist, a historic or political figure, an actor, or an artist? Would your mentor wear workout clothing and a gold medal around his or her neck? Would he or she wear spectacles, a military uniform, a sequined evening gown, or a three-piece suit? Take 10 minutes now to allow yourself to imagine a suitable mentor and expert in your chosen field. [Pause for 10 minutes.]

Now imagine yourself sitting with your inner mentor or guide. Discuss your personal feelings and questions about your chosen field and ask your mentor for any special insights into the topic. Envision this inner, back-and-forth discussion for about 20 minutes. If your mind draws a blank after a while, don't worry about it. Focus on your topic and your inner mentor until more images come to you and the inner dialogue picks up again. Continue with this part of the exercise for at least 20 minutes.

[20-minutes pause.]

Your inner journey with your mentor is about to come to a close for now. Before you take leave, however, acknowledge that you will be able to call upon your inner mentor whenever you need an alternative voice to help you through the terrain—the highest peaks, the lowest valleys, and the densest backwoods—of your learning experience. Remember, your inner mentor will always be there to raise the appropriate questions, to help you sort through the choices, to help you engage in a dialogue with your subject itself. Now wiggle your fingers and toes, open your eyes, and gradually bring yourself back to a state of ordinary waking awareness.

Hemispheric Hint—If you wish, you may think of your dream mentor before falling asleep. Incubating the presence of your dream mentor in your dreams may further enhance the skill of right-brain learning. Remember to tap dream-recollection techniques immediately upon waking up.

DAY 10

FANTASIA

The accounting student we discussed in our introduction was able to recognize the underlying patterns of accounting because he managed to "merge" with his subject. On Day 10, you'll practice a visualization exercise designed to help you deliberately induce a similar sense of inner connectedness with your chosen field.

Hemispheric Hint—Because some preparation is required, please read through all the instructions for Day 10 before you begin.

Set aside about an hour of time during which you will not be interrupted, then enter your right-brain refuge and choose a comfortable spot in which you can relax. Make sure that you have two tools with you: your "Under the Volcano" tape and an additional recording of baroque music that you can play after the "Volcano" tape has run its course.

First enter your right-brain refuge and sit down in a comfortable spot. Then play your "Under the Volcano" tape with baroque music. When this tape has run its course, sustain your state of alert relaxation as you put on your long-playing baroque tape or CD. But now, instead of just allowing your brain to drift, focus your thoughts on a specific image or object.

Once you feel relaxed, focus your thoughts on some object or mental image that has unique relevance to your field of study. If you are studying cell biology, for example, you might turn your thoughts toward a single cell. Envision the elaborate cell structures, from the swirling pulse of the tiny cellular hairs called cilia to the movement of vesicles that carry food through cell organelles to the cell's central command post—the nucleus itself.

If you are studying ice hockey, on the other hand, you might focus on the puck. If you are studying auto repair, you might focus on the engine, the carburetor, or the brakes. And if you are studying marine biology, you might envision tiny ocean plankton, a great white whale, or sulfurous jets of gas at the bottom of the sea.

You may choose virtually any object or image at all. There is just one limitation: Do not imagine yourself to be a person. In fact, even if your field is largely concerned with studying human interactions—such as history, psychology, or anthropology—you will get far more out of this exercise if you imagine yourself to be a geographic area, a biological structure (as opposed to a whole organism), or an inanimate object. We all have preconceived notions about people. On the other hand, imagining that you're an object encourages your imagination to stretch beyond any preset mental pictures you may have about your chosen subject.

By focusing on how it feels to be an electrode delivering a shock to a rat in a maze, for example, you should find yourself more deeply exploring complex concepts than if you were to simply imagine yourself as the rat. Most of us have biased cartoon images of what life must be like for a laboratory rat, but few of us have stopped to consider what it might be like to be a food pellet waiting to be eaten by the rat, or even to be the maze itself.

Once you have chosen a suitable object for your fantasy, and imagined yourself becoming that object, silently ask yourself questions about the ways in which you might experience reality from that object's point of view. If you are the guillotine, Williams suggests, for example, you might ask yourself how it feels to be chopping off hundreds of heads. How do you feel about the cheering crowds that continually feed you new victims? How do you feel when your victim is a six-year-old girl? How do you feel six months later, when you find yourself beheading some of those who once dragged other victims before you? By allowing your conscious imagination to stimulate your underlying thought processes in this fashion, you should find yourself gaining new and deeper insights into your chosen subject. Continue this phase of the exercise until your long-playing baroque music tape or CD comes to an end. As you complete your fantasy, be sure to allow yourself a sense of closure by gradually focusing your thoughts on your usual experience of yourself as you exist within everyday reality.

When the music has come to an end, turn your attention back to the details of the world around you. Wiggle your fingers and toes, open your eyes, and return to a state of complete waking consciousness.

Hemispheric Hint—Remember to keep up with the dream-learning techniques of the first two weeks. Each night before you go to bed think of the subject you are studying. In the morning, as soon as you wake up, practice the dream-recollection techniques described earlier.

DAY 11

THE INSIDE VIEW

On Day 11 you will take yesterday's exercise one step further. After you have "merged" with your chosen object or image, you will then imagine yourself detaching from it. Detached, but still mentally inside the image, you will envision it from a totally different point of view. For instance, if you are studying cell biology, you might imagine yourself as a tiny observer quietly watching a stream of sodium and potassium ions flowing through a cell membrane. If you are studying geometry, you might imagine yourself inside various geometric figures, examining them from all sides. Or, like the accounting student described in our introduction, you might imagine yourself surrounded by numbers and images that represent the overriding patterns of the subject itself.

To do the "Inside View" exercise for Day 11, start as you did on Day 10. Simply enter your right-brain refuge with the "Under the Volcano" tape, plus an additional hour of recorded baroque music. Enter a state of alert relaxation. Then, put on your long-playing music selection. Finally, when the long-playing recording is in progress, imagine that you are the same object or image that you invoked yesterday. As you did yesterday, imagine how it feels to be a cell, an ocean, or a guillotine.

But about halfway through the session, we'd like you to consciously shift the focus of your mental images. First, focus on altering your perspective so that you now view yourself back in your body, your sense of self completely intact. Then, envision yourself inside the thing you are studying. Remember, you are no longer one with this object or image. You are simply inside it. If you are inside the ocean, for instance, imagine the puffs of seaweed floating overhead like a blanket of vast green forest. Glimpse schools of goldfish swimming by you, envision a great white shark. If you are inside a series of geometric shapes, envision the sharp right angles of the cube, or the soft regular curve of the circle. If you are inside the human body, picture yourself traveling, helter-skelter, through the bloodstream toward the beating heart, the acidic sea of the small intestines, or the nerve-rich arena of the brain.

Picture the shape and texture, the internal workings and rhythms, of the object you are now inhabiting. Experience the luxury of a mental journey that is as rich and complex as possible.

Allow yourself another fifteen minutes for this second phase of imaging. After your fantasy winds down, however, be sure to give yourself a sense of closure by focusing on your usual experience of yourself as you exist within everyday reality. Then wiggle your fingers and toes, open your eyes, and gradually bring yourself back to an ordinary state of waking awareness.

DAY 12

CREATIVE
CLAYING

Before you begin the exercise for Day 12, go to the five-and-ten or hobby shop and buy some clay. Any type of clay, from real modeling clay to Play-Doh, will do. The important thing is that you have enough clay to fill both of your hands.

Hemispheric Hint—Read the rest of the instructions for Day 12 before continuing with the exercise.

After you have purchased your clay, spend at least thirty minutes immersed in your chosen topic. If you are studying organic chemistry, read the textbook (in your right-brain refuge or elsewhere) or work in the lab. If you are studying French, read a French novel or visit a French-speaking friend or a French bakery and have a conversation. You might even do something as conventionally left brain as attending an organic chemistry lecture or French workshop.

Then, after you have taken this straightforward, left-brain approach toward your subject, return to your right-brain refuge, dim the lights, and play your "Under the Volcano" tape together with the baroque music. Keep a couple of handfuls of clay by your side.

After you have entered the state of alert relaxation, put on your long-playing baroque music selection and, as you did on Day 10, imagine yourself to be an image or object related to your chosen field. Continue this visualization exercise for about fifteen minutes.

Then, as you did on Day 11, shift the focus of your attention so that you envision yourself not as the object or image itself, but rather, as a particle of awareness within it. Stick with this portion of the visualization for approximately fifteen minutes more.

Finally, take an ample quantity of clay in your hands and shift your focus once again. This time, shift your awareness so that you are no longer inside the object or image, but outside it looking in. As you examine the image in your mind's eye, take the clay and begin to sculpt the object or image in as much detail as possible. Try not to be analytical about this project. Simply focus on the image in your mind, and let that image emerge directly through your hands.

Continue to work with the clay for at least fifteen minutes. Then, when you feel ready, wiggle your toes, open your eyes, and return to a state of ordinary waking consciousness.

> **Hemispheric Hint**—Continue to incubate dreams about your chosen topic and use dream-recollection techniques in the morning. Also, please remember to continue to work on your topic in the more conventional, left-brain modes as the Whole Mind Program progresses.

DAY 13

THE INTUITIVE
CHUCKLE

We owe some of our most successful learning experiences to the wonderful role that humor plays in our lives. There is something about a well-chosen cartoon, comment, or joke that seems to loosen up our creative juices and make us feel more at home with a new and difficult field of study. We still fondly remember cramming for high school finals with friends, for example, and turning the subject matter into memorable phrases said to one another with exaggerated foreign accents and colorful innuendos that seemed impossible to forget. We still remember some of those answers twenty years later! There is also something almost sacred about our favorite cartoons that seem to capture our various fields of study on an almost intuitive level.

It is our opinion, in fact, that there is a kind of humor barrier that must be traversed before learning can become truly instinctive and intuitive on every level. You may have noticed, for instance, that you often begin making jokes about a particular subject only after you feel some sense of inner comfort toward it. Indeed, the very act of "lightening up" around a particular topic can actually ease the process of learning by overcoming any built-in resistance you may feel toward new information. It is almost as though it is okay to learn, once it becomes okay to laugh.

Of course, not every topic easily lends itself to humor. A Marine recruit learning to kill an opponent with his bare hands, or a paramedic trainee learning cardiopulmonary resuscitation, may rightfully feel that such matters of life and death are not even a little funny. Yet even these individuals may find it helpful to release the tension of the day's serious activities, during some appropriate break in the action, with a little humor. Even gallows humor may be an effective means of establishing a stronger intuitive connection to any given subject.

A case in point is the classic line handed to beginning scuba students worried about the possibility of encountering sharks. Addressing the student's fears, the instructor points out that he carries a knife as part of his underwater gear. The student inevitably asks how the instructor intends to fight off a shark with a tiny knife. The instructor then explains, "I'm not planning on fighting off the shark. I'm planning on cutting you open and distracting the shark with your blood while I head for the surface!" The student, of course, quickly learns that the instructor is not overly concerned about encountering sharks—which are rarely a threat for most divers.

On Day 13, you'll turn your own creative energies toward the lighter side of your chosen subject. Begin by going on a scavenger hunt for some cartoons about your topic. Then hang these cartoons in a suitable spot in your right-brain refuge.

> **Hemispheric Hint**—You might find some appropriate cartoons in magazines like *The New Yorker*, in book-length cartoon collections, or even around your instructor's office. Fellow students might have some good cartoons handy as well.

Once you have collected at least half a dozen cartoon favorites and have hung them on the wall in your right-brain refuge, spend some time alone enjoying the cartoons. What makes them especially funny to anyone familiar with your chosen field? Does the cartoonist capture something unique about the attitudes and behavior of those who frequent your area of study? Do the cartoons express something you've wanted to say yourself but could never quite voice?

Once you have had at least a few good laughs over some appropriate cartoons relating to your field, and have considered the source of their underlying humor, it's time to take a more lyrical focus. For part two of today's exercise, you should make up some humorous lyrics dealing with your field, to be sung to the tune of some popular song. Here's an example, written by Keith Harary, who happened to be studying biblical history. His lyrics describe the exodus of the Jews from Egypt, and should be sung to the tune of "Everything's Coming Up Roses":

> Part the sea with one hand.
> Step across like you're walkin' on land.
> Burn a bush. Have ten plagues.
> Baby, everything's comin' up Moses!
>
> Cross the desert alone.
> Build an ark in your spare time at home.
> Manna falls. Rivers flow.
> Baby, everything's comin' up Moses!
>
> Mark the doorposts in red.
> Tell the Pharaoh the first born are dead.
> Don't use yeast in the bread.
> Baby, everything's comin' up Moses!

That should give you some idea of what we mean. The idea in writing the lyrics for your particular song is to be as overtly outrageous and silly as possible, while still being entirely true to the underlying facts and subtleties of your chosen subject. The process of writing a song that is true to your particular field, yet still humorous, of course requires some real familiarity with your topic. If you share this exercise with a friend who is also studying the same subject, you may find yourselves teaching each other some of the more subtle points of your field. You don't have to write an entire song, of course. A couple of good verses should suffice.

Hemispheric Hint—Remember to incubate dreams related to your topic of study each night, and to use dream-recollection techniques the first thing each morning.

DAY 14

LUCID DREAMING
101

By now you should have been practicing dream-recall and dream-incubation techniques on a nightly basis for more than a week. You should, therefore, be ready to try a more advanced exercise designed to assist you in deliberately inducing *lucid dreams*—dreams in which you're aware that you're dreaming, even though you're fast asleep. Lucid dreaming can aid the learning experience by enabling you to consciously explore your topic of interest while your right brain is running the show—that is, while you are having a dream. The lucid-dream technique can be particularly valuable to the learning process if it motivates you to continue to explore your inner experiences and right-brain impressions while awake.

To have a lucid dream, you must, of course, recognize that you are dreaming. One way to accomplish this is to ask yourself if you are asleep and dreaming as you go about the day. Therefore, begin Day 14 much as you normally do. Eat some breakfast, for instance, then go about your errands or drive to work. But every twenty minutes or so, stop, look around you, and ask yourself: *Is this a dream?* Let's say you're taking the subway from your apartment to your downtown firm:

First study the people around you. Do they have normal, everyday faces? Or does that slim young woman to your left boast two heads? What about the billboard to your left? Read the ad on it once, then read it again. Was the material you read each time different or the same? If the words differed from one reading to the next, and you're not looking at some changeable electronic sign, you are in a dream. Now, as you enter your office, study the details there, too. For instance, does the view out of your window include the same megaliths and highways as usual? Or do you now see a scene from prehistoric times complete with dinosaurs and giant ferns, a street scene in Camelot, or an underwater city on the bottom of the ocean? If the scenery is somehow askew, you are in a dream.

One of the best ways to see whether or not you're in a dream is to try to change part of your setting through ''thought'' alone. Here's an example: Let's say your waiter brings you a chicken pot pie. Before you take a bite, look at the plate and will the chicken pot pie into a T-bone steak. If the transformation takes place, you are most certainly in a dream. Continue to ask, *Is this a dream*? throughout the day. Then answer your question with an appropriate reality check.

Remember: You can usually recognize a dream through the occurence of anything weirdly inappropriate or bizarre. For instance, if you suddenly find yourself sporting a long, fluffy tail; if you are walking around completely naked in front of the Lincoln Memorial and don't know how you got there; if you find yourself confronting an especially red individual who breathes fire, carries a pitchfork, and laughs like a demon; or if you dine on the barbecued flesh of a local politician or encounter the giant from Jack in the Beanstalk, you are probably (we can only hope) having a dream. If feelings and thoughts seem oddly inconsistent, if the structure of reality is constantly shifting, you are probably in a dream. Then again, you may simply be losing your marbles.

If your frequent reality checks tell you that your are not in a dream, remind yourself that you are, instead, awake and conscious of everything going on. Every time you discover that you are awake, say, *This is not a dream*. Then focus on the sensation of being conscious and wide awake.

Finally, before you go to bed, tell yourself, *Tonight I will recognize that I am dreaming while in the midst of my dream*. Write this sentence in your dream journal before you place the book beside your bed. Then, repeat the sentence again as you drift off to sleep. Remember, you can perform the same reality checks in your dreams that you now regularly perform during the day.

If you should happen to awaken after a dream in the middle of the night, stop to consider what was dreamlike about it. Then, repeat the sentence, *Tonight I will recognize that I am dreaming while in the midst of my dream*, and fall back to sleep.

Tomorrow morning, during the early hours, you are likely to awaken spontaneously from a nonlucid dream. When you do, lie in bed quietly, neither moving nor opening your eyes, and think about your dream. Go over it in your mind in as much detail as possible, absorbing the setting, the characters, the imagery, and the plot. Review the dream several times, until you have committed it to memory.

Then, while you are preparing to go back to sleep, tell yourself, *The next time I have a dream, I will recognize that I am dreaming*. Now play the tape of the dream through the video recorder of your brain, visualizing each detail as fully and richly as you can. However, add one element that was clearly missing before: This time, as you replay the dream, view it as if you, the dreamer, are conscious of the dream as it is going on. Then repeat the tag phrase, *The next time I have a dream, I will recognize that I am dreaming*. Repeat these two steps until you fall asleep.

If you follow these instructions, you should find yourself falling backward from your near-conscious state into the realm of dreams. You may find yourself replaying the dream you just left, or generating a whole new dream. Either way, if you have been successful, you may find yourself in the midst of a lucid dream.

For Day 14, you should simply practice the lucid-dream technique without tying it in to right-brain learning. But as you progress through the Whole Mind Program, in the days and weeks that follow, you will also use lucid dreaming to enhance your ability to learn.

Hemispheric Hint—Each night before you go to bed and as you are drifting off to sleep, quietly vow to remember your dreams. If you wake up from a dream in the middle of the night, try to fall back into a lucid dream. Also, remember to record your dreams and lucid dreams in your dream journal on a daily basis.

Hemispheric Hint—Practicing dream recall, dream incubation, and lucid dreaming can take you a long way toward communicating with the inner part of yourself accessible primarily through your dreams. Many people, in fact, have reported that these dream-awareness techniques have helped them to solve personal problems, boost their immunity, and even enhance their careers. Once this communication link with your own inner self has been established, you should also be able to use your dreams, especially lucid dreams, to enhance your underlying sense of openness toward any subject. Once that happens, your openness to your subject—and your ability to learn—will be enhanced.

Hemispheric Hint—Do not neglect to study your topic in the more conventional, left-brain mode, even as you begin to master these right-brain learning techniques. Remember, it's important to learn with both parts of your brain if you hope to penetrate your topic on every level.

In any event, congratulations are in order! You've just completed Week Two of the Whole Mind Program!

WEEK TWO MAKE A RIGHT AT MAGIC MOUNTAIN

DAY 8 LEARNING IN DREAMTIME	DAY 9 THE INNER MENTOR

DAY 8 — LEARNING IN DREAMTIME

Decorate your dream room with favorite objects that express the most positive aspects of your personality and important dimensions of your chosen field.

Place your dream diary, special pen, and penlight in a prominent spot beside the bed.

Focus on your chosen subject, excluding all other thoughts from your mind.

Just before going to sleep, articulate the topic of your prospective dream. Using your special pen, write the phrase in your dream diary. Then turn off the lights and go to sleep.

As you fall asleep, focus on the phrase and picture the special objects you've placed around you in the room. Remind yourself to dream about the subject at hand and to remember all related dreams when you wake up.

Practice dream-recollection techniques and record your dreams in your journal immediately after opening your eyes.

DAY 9 — THE INNER MENTOR

Choose a comfortable spot where you can relax, in your right-brain refuge or some suitable nearby location.

Arrange to have 60 to 90 minutes of baroque music playing in the background.

Play your "Under the Volcano" tape, with the added selection of baroque music, and enter a state of alert relaxation.

After you have spent 20 to 30 minutes in a state of alert relaxation, have a friend read the guided imagery script for Day 9. If a friend is unable to participate, make a tape recording of the script and simply play it back in your tape recorder after the "Under the Volcano" tape is complete.

Follow the guided imagery instructions.

Later, as you are falling asleep, incubate the presence of your dream mentor in your dreams.

Remember to apply the dream-recollection techniques you've learned upon waking up and to record your dreams in your dream diary.

DAY 10 FANTASIA		**DAY 11** THE INSIDE VIEW	
Listen to your "Under the Volcano" tape with baroque music and enter a state of alert relaxation. Put on your long-playing baroque tape or CD. Focus your thoughts on some image or object that has a unique relevance to your chosen field. Imagine yourself becoming that object, and silently ask yourself questions about the ways in which you might experience reality from that object's point of view. Continue this phase of the exercise until your long-playing ba-	roque music tape or CD comes to an end. As you complete your fantasy, allow yourself a sense of closure by gradually focusing your thoughts on your usual experience of yourself as you exist within everyday reality. Return to a state of complete waking consciousness.	Enter your right-brain refuge and choose a comfortable spot in which to relax. Listen to your "Under the Volcano" tape with baroque music and enter a state of alert relaxation. Play your long-playing baroque tape or CD. Focus your thoughts on the same image or ojbect that you chose for Day 10, this time imagining that you are inside of the thing you are studying. For 15 minutes, picture the shape and texture, the internal workings and rhythms, of the object	you imagine yourself inhabiting.

WEEK TWO MAKE A RIGHT AT MAGIC MOUNTAIN
(continued)

DAY 12 CREATIVE CLAYING		DAY 13 THE INTUITIVE CHUCKLE	DAY 14 LUCID DREAMING 101	
Buy enough clay to fill your two hands.

Spend 30 minutes immersed in your chosen topic.

Return to your right-brain refuge, dim the lights, and listen to your "Under the Volcano" tape with baroque music. Enter a state of alert relaxation.

Play your long baroque music selection and, for 15 minutes imagine yourself as an image or object related to your chosen field.

Shift your focus so that, for the next 15 minutes, you see yourself inside the object or image. | Take an ample quantity of clay in both hands and shift your focus so that you visualize yourself looking in at your chosen object or image from the outside.

Close your eyes and sculpt the object or image in clay with as much detail as possible for at least 15 minutes.

Return to a state of ordinary waking awareness. | Go on a scavenger hunt for some cartoons about your chosen field. Hang these cartoons in your right-brain refuge.

Spend some time alone studying the cartoons and considering their relation to your area of study.

Make up some humorous lyrics dealing with your field to be sung to the tune of some popular song. | Begin Day 14 much as you normally do, but every 20 minutes or so, stop, look around you, and ask yourself: *Is this a dream?*

If your frequent reality checks tell you that you are not dreaming, remind yourself that you are instead awake and conscious of everything going on. Every time you discover that you are awake, tell yourself, *This is not a dream.* Then focus on the sensation of being conscious and wide awake.

Before you go to bed, tell yourself, *Tonight I will* | |

recognize that *I am dreaming while in the midst of my dream*. Write this sentence in your dream journal. Then repeat this sentence again as you drift off to sleep.

Remember that you can perform the same reality checks in your dreams that you now regularly perform during the day.

If you should happen to awaken after a dream in the middle of the night, stop to consider what was dreamlike about it. Then, repeat to yourself the sentence, *Tonight I will recognize that I am dreaming while in the midst of* *my dream*, and fall back to sleep.

If you find yourself awakening spontaneously from a nonlucid dream, lie in bed quietly, and think about your dream in as much detail as possible, absorbing the setting, characters, imagery, and plot. Review the dream several times, until you have committed it to memory.

While you are preparing to fall back asleep, tell yourself, *The next time I have a dream, I will recognize that I am dreaming*. Envision yourself in the midst of the previous dream, but this time as being aware of it while it's happening. Repeat these two steps until you fall asleep.

WEEK THREE

THE YIN AND YANG OF LEARNING

WEEK THREE

•

THE YIN AND YANG
OF LEARNING

As we have continually tried to point out, right-brain learning cannot replace the conventional methods of learning you have relied on throughout your life. Rather, right-brain techniques should be used in conjunction with more conventional forms of learning for optimum success.

In Week Three of the Whole Mind Program, you will learn to integrate right- and left-brain techniques so that an appropriately balanced learning style results. This segment of the Whole Mind Program is especially important following Weeks One and Two, in which you turned down the volume of the left brain so that the power of the right brain could emerge. In the first two weeks, intensive right-brain work was the key. But in Week Three, you will once more turn up the volume of the left brain so that it can work in harmony with the right.

In one exercise, for instance, you will learn the technique of tunneling, in which you establish new lines of communication between the right hemisphere and the left. Tapping this technique, you will use your right brain's power of visualization to envision the left-brain task of hitting the books.

In other Week Three exercises, you will apply right-brain skills to the notoriously left-brain task of writing. In one such exercise, you will use a technique called clustering, in which you chart your topic, creating unique and spontaneous patterns that may help you understand your topic holistically for the first time. In another Week Three exercise, you will create written images—metaphors—that parallel the visual pictures you created in Weeks One and Two.

Finally, your right and left modes of thinking will meet with the help of experiential learning—a technique that asks you to experience, in as real-life a manner as possible, the subject at hand. That means if you're studying marine biology, you'll go scuba diving; if you're studying cosmology, you'll go to an observatory or planetarium to look through the telescope or sit in the darkness under the stars. Since not all topics are accessible so directly, you will also be able to experience your topic through the media of movies, museum exhibits, and exhibitions at aquariums, botanical gardens, or zoos.

As you work your way through Week Three, you will come to understand the value of multifaceted, multisensory, multidimensional learning. In learning, as in everything else, the art of balance, the yin and yang, will stand you in good stead.

DAY 15

LUCID-DREAM LEARNING

On Day 15 you will learn to use lucid dreaming to enhance the learning process while you sleep. To do so, first continue with the reality checks introduced on Day 14. As you go about your day, continue to examine everyday reality for any signs that you might be in a dream.

During Day 15, we suggest that you spend some time letting your thoughts roam freely, without pressure, over your creative or intellectual pursuits. Calmly tell yourself that you will come to a new, deeper, more profound understanding of the subject matter in your dreams.

Then, about an hour before you plan to go to bed, gather a few objects that symbolize some significant aspects of your chosen field. These incubation objects should be added to any others you may have placed in your sleeping environment earlier in the Whole Mind Program. You might, for example, choose a a catcher's mitt, a bat, and a pack of trading cards to symbolize your interest in baseball; an assortment of bandages, antiseptics, and painkillers to symbolize your interest in medicine; or a camera, some extra lenses, and several rolls of film to symbolize your interest in photography.

Place these objects near your bedside and casually contemplate their symbolic significance in relation to your field. (The more matter-of-factly you approach this technique, the more likely it is to be successful.) You might also consider enhancing the atmosphere by introducing an appropriate scent—such as a flowery perfume to represent gardening, or a musk scent to represent the Far East—or by playing music in the background. You may play either baroque music or a soothing kind of music that is symbolic of your field. For instance, if you're studying the era of the Sixties, you might consider some of the songs of John Lennon or the Doors.

When you're ready, get into bed and write an incubation phrase in your dream diary that expresses some overall concern you have about your chosen subject. If you have been having a problem understanding some part of the material you've been reviewing, gently focus on those ideas that you have found the most confusing. Then turn out the lights, relax, and allow yourself to drift off to sleep.

Gently focus on entering a lucid dream state just as you did on Day 14 with the tag phrase, *The next time I have a dream, I will recognize that I am dreaming.* As you drift off to sleep, focus your thoughts on the most fascinating aspects of your subject and on your need to gain special insights into your field. Of course, it is important not to focus so intensely on any of these ideas that you'll keep yourself awake.

> **Hemispheric Hint**—Remember, you may wake up from a nonlucid dream in the middle of the night. If you do so, simply play back the dream in your mind. But this time, add two details: some aspect of your chosen subject and the image of yourself being conscious of the dream as it occurs. You may well fall back into a lucid dream.

> **Hemispheric Hint**—If the matter upon which you have chosen to focus is important, then, on some level at least, you've already been thinking about it. In fact, given your increasing familiarity with the subject matter of your chosen field, you probably already possess subtle, perhaps even unconscious, clues to the answers you seek. All you must really do, then, is go on a kind of vision quest—that is, allow your experience, knowledge, and creative energy to merge in a moment of intuitive vision that takes the form of a dream.
>
> You may find this focus generating a dream or lucid dream that reflects your ongoing inner learning process. On the other hand, you may simply wake up in the morning with a deeper sense of clarity toward your overall learning experience.

If all goes well, of course, you will have a lucid dream that deals directly with your concerns. If you should find yourself actually having this compelling experience, we suggest that you use it to explore your own inner relationship with your subject, and to resolve any creative or conceptual roadblocks facing you.

As an undergraduate psychology student, for example, one friend of ours used lucid dreaming to gain a deeper understanding of behavioral psychology, a topic he found too mundane to relate to in a personal way. His immediate problem: He was supposed to write an original paper on this topic, though it was one that he didn't find particularly enthralling. After spending much of a day considering his assignment, he finally decided to go to sleep in the hope of inducing a lucid dream on the desired topic. Sure enough, just before waking up in the morning, he found himself experiencing an intense lucid dream in which he was a rat in a specially designed box. As he ran through the box, he intentionally modified various aspects of his environment by operating a complex assortment of levers and switches. He committed a drawing of the box to paper the moment he woke up, and spent the rest of the morning writing a term paper based upon the underlying concept. Ironically, the professor who gave the paper an ''A'' was an exceptionally conservative behavioral psychologist not known for being favorably disposed toward studies of altered states of consciousness. He was never told that the term paper he viewed so highly had emerged directly out of a lucid dream.

Hemispheric Hint—Remember to practice dream-recollection techniques when you first wake up and to write down any and all impressions of your remembered dreams as quickly as possible. You may be surprised to find that specific images, words, ideas, or metaphors that relate to your creative concerns in a powerful way. You may even wake up with an apparent solution or some special insight—even if you can't consciously relate this inspirational artifact to a specific dream.

Hemispheric Hint—Remember, any creative ideas or images that emerge from incubated dreams must be carefully evaluated from the perspective of rational, waking consciousness. You may find yourself initially inspired by your dream experience, only to realize, later in the day, that it requires further development. On the other hand, you may be delighted to find yourself reaching full waking awareness with a completely formed and coherent mental image, idea, or impression that is directly applicable to your immediate needs—especially if you practice creative dream incubation in conjunction with lucid dreaming on a regular basis. The lucid-dream environment, in particular, can provide a subjective sense of distance from your waking concerns that can help you gain fresh insights into your chosen subject.

DAY 16

TUNNELING

As we have emphasized throughout the past fifteen days of the Whole Mind Program, right-brain learning cannot be done in a vacuum. In order to fully comprehend almost any topic, the left brain must also be deeply involved in the learning process. Indeed, the right-brain exercises within this book should never prevent your left brain from reading the appropriate texts, writing the appropriate essays, or analyzing, as only your left brain can, the subject at hand. Nonetheless, just to make sure that your right brain continues to work in tandem with your left, we present the tunneling exercise below. It is only when the two aspects of mental functioning cooperate in the learning process that an optimal learning experience can occur.

The tunneling exercise is meant to help you create a "tunnel of communication" between your right and left brain. Think of the phenomenon as analogous to tunneling electrons, which, because of their special properties, can literally penetrate matter, tunneling from one side of a solid object to the next.

To begin this exercise, enter your right-brain refuge and induce a state of alert relaxation.

> **Hemispheric Hint**—You may enter the state of alert relaxation, as you have in the past, while playing your "Under the Volcano" tape. Or if you now feel reasonably skilled at the technique, you may simply skip the tape and spend about five minutes visualizing mental energy traveling through your body and relaxing one muscle after the next.

Once you are totally relaxed, visualize yourself effectively studying your chosen subject. Visualize the place and time in which you will study, and even the clothes you are likely to wear. For example, you may decide to sit at your kitchen table in jeans and a T-shirt and study calculus for an hour beginning at 7:00 P.M. Imagine the kitchen clock showing that exact time, and visualize yourself walking over to the table, sitting down, picking up the calculus book, and maintaining a relaxed, alert focus as you study the concepts presented in the text.

It is not necessary—or even desirable—to analyze any of the specific concepts you'll later be encountering during your actual study session. Instead, just imagine yourself feeling generally upbeat and interested as you explore your chosen subject. Be sure to keep your focus positive:

Don't imagine yourself "not feeling frustrated," because associating frustration with learning is a negative message to give your subconscious. Even if you tend to find the subject matter you'll be studying particularly opaque or unenthralling, this exercise can still help you set a more positive subconscious frame of reference for your future learning experience.

Complete this exercise by studying your chosen subject at the time and place you imagined during your visualization experience. Remember the sense of focus and calm that you envisioned for yourself during the relaxation exercise. Allow yourself to draw upon this inner image of yourself successfully studying the material at hand.

As an effective variation, you may practice this visualization exercise while in a deeply relaxed state just prior to falling asleep or right after waking up.

DAY 17

RIGHT-BRAIN
WRITING

Now that you have begun to forge a tunnel of communication between the right and left brain, you can take that interplay one step further with clustering—a writing technique that enables you to combine the organizational ability of the left brain with the rapid-fire associations of the right. In essence, the clustering technique enables you to rewrite the long lists of facts and externally imposed linear concepts associated with your subject so that they make fluid, intuitive sense uniquely to you.

As our colleague, educator Gabriele Rico, author of *Writing the Natural Way*, has often pointed out, the only way to learn effectively is to transform somebody else's organization into your own inner pattern. This is as true of learning purely academic subjects, such as world history and economics, as it is of learning in more hands-on fields, such as blacksmithing or truck driving.

The student who miraculously passed his accounting exam by suddenly perceiving a pattern in the diagrams in his textbook, for example, succeeded not because he was able instantly to absorb an entire semester's worth of information, but because he was able to preceive a pattern that was uniquely meaningful to him. Had he tried to explain his personal concept of that pattern to other people, it might not have worked as well for them. On the other hand, they might have taken his reported experience as an inspiration to discover their own inner patterns in the material at hand.

To actively facilitate such pattern recognition, Rico developed "clustering," an approach she claims allows you to absorb information, in any field, from ten to fifty times faster than you otherwise would. A cluster is simply a rapidly produced graphic representation of the patterns you perceive in relation to various words and concepts as you progress through the learning process. On Day 17, you'll begin practicing Rico's clustering technique.

By clustering, Rico says, you'll be setting up a mental pattern that can later serve as a holistic frame of reference for future learning. Indeed, says Rico, learning is often a fragmented process in which we frantically try to memorize and understand things without a global context. Rico has found, however, that creating a cluster allows you to create your own mental context for the subject at hand. It allows you to find out what you already know and what you don't know about the topic, and also allows you to juggle ideas so that one association begets the next. Even when you've done only your first cluster, therefore, you've activated your mind and are focused in a way that wouldn't have been possible if you had just sat down and said, "I want to learn about auto mechanics."

To practice clustering, you'll need a blank piece of paper, a pen or pencil, and at least half a dozen different-colored felt-tip pens. To create a cluster, begin by writing the name of your topic in the middle of the piece of paper, then drawing a circle around what you've written. If you're studying auto mechanics, for example, simply write down and circle the words "auto mechanics." Then let your thoughts roam freely and jot down any ideas and associations that come to mind. You may also draw quick and simple pictures to symbolize your concepts.

Place these words and pictures anywhere on the page that feels appropriate, circling them as you go along, and making no effort to deliberately organize them. You might, for example, find yourself writing down such things as car, engine, oil, wrenches, and battery. You might draw a picture of a can of gasoline or a set of tires. As you do so, you should begin to discover that you know much more about auto mechanics than you previously thought. The initial free-association process involved in creating the cluster soon becomes a self-organizing process and a pattern begins to emerge.

When you run out of words and pictures, you'll find yourself with a graphic representation of the concepts you associate with a particular topic. At this point, you should use the colored pens to draw lines between the various circled words, connecting those concepts that seem to belong together in the same colors, and allowing the incipient patterns within your cluster to graphically emerge. You may, for example, use a red pen to connect those concepts that have to do with a car's electrical system, blue to connect words relating to the engine, and so forth.

> ***Hemispheric Hint***—After you've carried out this simple exercise, study your chosen subject for at least an hour. Continue making similar clusters for each subsequent chapter you encounter as you read about your field.

> ***Hemispheric Hint***—If you are also attending classes, Rico suggests, you should take the time to make a cluster at the end of each class before leaving the classroom. By creating a one- or two-minute cluster out of all that was discussed in each class, the most important aspects of the talk will take on an organic organization and will not remain fragmented in your thoughts. You may wish to label your clusters and keep them together in a notebook, which Rico calls a "thought log," for later reference as you review your subject or prepare for a test.

> ***Hemispheric Hint***—You can even draw quick clusters before responding to the essay questions on an exam as a way of collecting your thoughts and formulating an organized response. According to Rico, students who have used this approach have often dramatically improved their grades. Reviewing a cluster also retriggers the inner pattern you experienced at the time it was drawn.

> ***Hemispheric Hint***—Continue to incubate lucid and nonlucid dreams on your field of interest, and to practice dream-recollection techniques upon first waking up in the morning.

DAY 18

READING FOR
POETS

Reading is usually a left-brain activity, since it requires attention to language, linear detail, and analytic thought. However, applying a bit of right-brain magic to your reading activities can help you understand your subject with far more potency and acumen than you did before. Particularly when you are working with a text that is dry and technical, or extremely rigid in its approach, a right-brain perspective can facilitate your grasp of the author's message and point of view. In fact, you might think of the right-brain reading exercise that follows as a sort of "reading for poets"—that is, you will attempt to take even the driest, most technical text and view it with the sensual, rhythmic, visual sensibility you apply to the reading of poems.

To apply right-brain reading to your field of interest, simply take the text or texts with which you are working and flip through them randomly, looking at the various chapter headings and noticing whether patterns begin to emerge. (Remember, you can use this technique whether your topic is English literature, refrigerator repair, or horticulture.) Then spend about thirty minutes randomly reading any segments that catch your interest. Especially look at any pictures, charts, or graphs that explain the topic as a whole. As soon as your interest in one area flags, go on to the next.

This simple activity should give you a rough, but intuitive, overview of the literature in your field. After the thirty-minute right-brain reading session, take out the clustering tools you used yesterday and proceed to create a cluster based on your experience. After you have finished your cluster, contemplate how it relates to the overall patterns of your book or books.

Hemispheric Hint—If reading is not one of the tools you use to study your subject, then just spend the day immersed in your topic on whatever level you choose. After you have studied your subject to your satisfaction, spend 20 to 30 minutes organizing the day's activities in your mind through clustering.

Hemispheric Hint—Continue to incubate lucid and nonlucid dreams on your field of interest and to practice dream-recollection techniques upon waking up in the morning.

DAY 19

MIXED
METAPHORS

Today you will expand on the right-brain writing exercise of Day 17 by creating what we call "mixed metaphors"—that is, metaphors that emerge as you mix the intellectual skills of the right brain with those of the left. After all, creating a truly meaningful metaphor means enlisting your powers of language (a left-brain skill) and visualization (a right-brain skill). "Mixed Metaphors," therefore, is the perfect exercise for Day 19, when you will be focusing on merging the powers of your left and right brains. Indeed, once you've begun absorbing a certain amount of information about your chosen field, creative metaphors can make the material you've been studying come alive in your imagination.

Hemispheric Hint—Because some preparation is required, please read the instructions that follow before you begin.

To begin the exercise for Day 19, spend from thirty minutes to an hour engaged in your chosen topic: You may read a book, do some writing, paint a picture, program a computer—whatever seems appropriate to the given subject matter. Then, if you are not already in your right-brain refuge, go there and assume a state of alert relaxation.

Hemispheric Hint—You may enter the state of alert relaxation while playing your "Under the Volcano" tape or simply by spending about five minutes visualizing mental energy traveling through your body and relaxing one muscle after the next.

As you feel yourself becoming more and more relaxed, allow any images you associate with your chosen field to spontaneously flow through your imagination. As you notice these images passing through your mind, search for metaphors with which to define your topic.

If you are studying astronomy, for example, you might say to yourself, *Astronomy is like a vast and three-dimensional game of cosmic billiards*. Then allow yourself to imagine the solar system as a gigantic three-dimensional billiard table, with the planets moving around like different-size balls in constant motion. If you are studying statistics, you might tell yourself, *Statistics is like sampling the number of different-colored jelly beans in a jar by pouring out a handful at a time.*

Let your imagination roam freely, and be as original as possible in the metaphor you choose. Whenever possible, this metaphor should reflect not only your chosen topic, but also your personal history or your current life. If your kitchen is infested with cockroaches, for example, and you are studying military strategy, you might think of military tactics in the context of an army of roaches invading your building. In another example, if you are studying internal medicine and are fascinated by auto mechanics, you might tell yourself that studying human physiology is like studying the internal workings of an automobile engine. Picture the human body as a series of tubes, filters, pipes, intakes, and exhausts.

Once you have arrived at a suitable metaphor for your field of interest, gradually allow yourself to return to a normal state of waking awareness. Take a break, then spend at least an hour playfully exploring the metaphor you've created firsthand. If your metaphor involves automobile mechanics, for example, you might spend some time working on your car or looking around a store that specializes in auto supplies and parts. You might even bring some part of an automobile engine home as a conversation piece for your coffee table. If it involves counting jelly beans, go out and get a giant jar of colored jelly beans for your right-brain refuge. If your metaphor involves insects, you might decide to buy yourself an ant farm.

DAY 20

SEEING THE
ELEPHANT

Nearly all of the education experts with whom we have spoken have pointed out that there is no substitute for direct experience in facilitating the learning process—and in getting the right brain and the left brain to work smoothly together. If you're studying botany, for example, your comprehension will be enhanced if you regularly spend time exploring a botanical garden, just as any study of elephants would be incomplete without a firsthand visit to the savannah, or at least the zoo. Your awareness of the broader context of any number of subjects, from anthropology to modern art, can also be significantly improved by exploring art galleries and museums. Indeed, a practical, hands-on experience can deepen your understanding of virtually any topic, and can certainly clarify your understanding of even the most seemingly esoteric or difficult aspects of your field.

On Day 20, therefore, you'll go on a field expedition to experience your chosen topic in the real world. For example, you might visit a psychiatric hospital, a newspaper, a fine art gallery, a French restaurant, a sewage treatment plant, or a military installation. Whatever real-life setting you select, be certain that it is one that will immerse you in your chosen field on as many sensory levels as possible.

Once you have arrived at an appropriate location, take an hour or so to explore your surroundings. Read all exhibit materials, for example, if you are visiting a museum and allow yourself to become completely absorbed in the exhibits themselves. If you are watching a sporting event, just enjoy it without necessarily analyzing the action on a conscious level. If you are visiting a psychiatric hospital, allow yourself to absorb the full impact of your experience on a personal level beyond the theoretical context of psychological and psychiatric texts.

After you have spent an hour or so informally exploring your surroundings, you're ready to practice a more intense exercise in right-brain sensory awareness. Begin by sitting quietly in a stimulating spot in your field trip location. As you sit, observe your surroundings without attracting any unnecessary attention. You might, for example, pick a bench in a corner of the museum, a back row in the concert hall or stadium, a table in the back of the restaurant, or the edge of a pier overlooking an armada of Navy ships in the harbor. Wherever you choose to be, make certain it is a location in which you can safely close your eyes and venture inward without putting yourself in any personal danger.

Get comfortable in the location you've chosen and allow yourself to relax without closing your eyes. It is not necessary or even desirable, for the purposes of this exercise, to enter a full-blown state of alert relaxation. Rather, you should relax enough to ''take the edge off'' any residual tension in your mind and body, while still remaining completely alert and fully aware of everything that is going on around you.

Take a deep breath and listen to the sound of your own breathing. Then, as you continue listening to yourself breathing slowly in and out, gradually expand your focus of attention to include the other sounds around you in your immediate environment. Keep your eyes open throughout this part of the exercise, but don't look around you at the sources of the sounds you're hearing unless this is absolutely necessary or unavoidable.

After a while, begin moving around your immediate surroundings on foot. As you move about, continue to pay close attention to the sound of your breathing and the other sounds you encounter in your environment. While concentrating on these sounds, try as much as possible to temporarily ignore any other nonauditory sensory experiences you may be having except, of course, those essential for safely navigating your environment. Again, avoid intentionally looking in the direction of any sounds you hear unless it is absolutely necessary to avoid an accident.

Pay attention to the layers of sound that surround you, and note how certain sounds draw your immediate attention while others seem to fade into the general background. Concentrate on the sounds that are closest to you, then on those that are farthest away. Then concentrate on the loudest or most dramatic sounds around you, followed by the softer and more subtle sounds that you usually don't consciously notice. Keep directing your attention toward all of the subtle and powerful sounds in the surrounding environment, until you're able comfortably to focus on any particular sound or sounds to which you choose to pay attention, while deliberately excluding other sounds from your immediate awareness. Then practice listening to various combinations of sounds, and to all the sounds around you at once, without losing track of the individual sounds you're hearing.

Spend a minimum of fifteen minutes practicing this sensory focusing exercise with your sense of hearing as your guide. Then return to the spot where you began focusing on your hearing, take a deep breath, and relax. Concentrate on any information that's coming to you through your sense of smell. Concentrate first on the familiar smell of your own body. Do you regularly wear perfume or cologne or anything else that gives you a recognizable scent? You may find that your sense of smell has become dulled to this familiar aroma. Shortly after you splash on cologne, for example, you may no longer notice it even though the others around you may notice the scent quite easily. Rub your palms on the part of you where the scent should be strongest, then hold your hands up to your nose and breathe deeply. Notice how the scent becomes stronger for a moment, then once again seems to fade.

Are there other familiar smells that you associate with your body? Smell your clothes, for example, and notice the scent of your detergent. If you're wearing a jacket or coat, does it smell different from the shirt or sweater you're wearing under it? Unbutton your top, or pull out the collar, and put your nose inside of it so that you can smell your skin. Does the inside of your shirt smell different from the outside?

Now turn your attention toward your immediate environment. Allow the familiar smells of your body to fade into the background of your awareness and notice the other immediate smells around you. Without closing your eyes, turning your head, or moving from your initial spot, what are the strongest smells you notice in your nearby surroundings? Do you smell the heady and unmistakable aroma of elephants walking around in their enclosure at the zoo? Do you smell the floor wax used in the museum, or the hot dogs and popcorn they sell at the athletic stadium?

When you feel ready, begin moving around the special location you've chosen for this exercise. As you move about, continue to focus on the variety of smells around you. Use your other senses to direct you toward as many interesting smells as possible, but don't just concentrate on those smells that are closest to you. Instead, as you did when you concentrated on your hearing, try to focus on a variety of smells at varying distances from your body. Use your own familiar smell as a reference point to focus your attention in more closely, then use distant smells to focus your attention farther and farther away. Notice how some smells seem to draw your immediate interest, while others are more subtle and seem to fade into the overall background of your environment or become overpowered by the stronger smells around you.

Spend a minimum of fifteen minutes focusing on your sense of smell in this fashion. Then take a fifteen- to twenty-minute break before moving on to the next phase of the exercise.

For the final phase of today's right-brain exercise in experiential learning, you'll combine your heightened sensory awareness with creative visualization. Once again, you should begin by relaxing in the field trip location you have chosen. Take a deep breath and slowly let it out. Then close your eyes and relax. (Once again, it is not necessary at this time to enter a complete state of alert relaxation.) As you feel yourself relaxing, imagine that you are in the very center of activity in the location you have chosen.

If you are at a hockey match, for example, imagine yourself skating across the ice in the center of the game. Feel the cold air circulating all around you, and listen to the sound of your imaginary skates and hockey stick as they scrape across the ice. If you are sitting at a harbor, imagine yourself on the deck of a ship, feeling the rumble of the engines reverberating through the hull and smelling the salty air blowing in your face.

> **Hemispheric Hint**—If you are at a museum, do not imagine yourself behind the scenes of the museum itself unless you are studying to become a curator of museum exhibits. Rather, you should imagine the exhibits themselves actually coming to life, with yourself at the center of the action. See yourself standing on an African plain, for example, smelling the dry grass and the pungent aroma of animals in the distance. Or imagine yourself in Renoir's studio in Paris, smelling the pigment of the paint and sipping strong, black coffee as you watch the artist at work.

Continue the combined visualization and sensory awareness phase of this exercise for at least another fifteen or twenty minutes. Then spend at least another hour exploring your field trip surroundings in whatever way you find appropriate.

DAY 21

MOTIF OF THE MOVING IMAGE

No matter what your subject, there's really no substitute for direct experience. But as far as we're concerned, direct experience can take many forms. For instance, if you're studying the Civil War, prehistoric life, or cosmology, a truly direct personal experience is hard to come by. And even if you can immerse yourself directly in your field—say you're studying contemporary Soviet civilization and you visit Moscow, or you're studying ice skating and you ice skate—you cannot experience your subject from every possible perspective or point of view.

To deepen the flavor of experiential learning, therefore, we suggest that you spend some time at the movies. Only in the movies can the beginning figure skater get swept up in the emotion of winning the Olympics; only in the movies can the cosmologist get swept up in the sensation of hurtling outward into the vast infinity of the cosmos itself.

The Civil War could almost seem to come alive, for example, by watching Ken Burns's remarkable television documentary, *The Civil War*, or by watching the Academy Award–winning feature film *Glory*. Prehistoric life might seem to come alive by watching such feature films as *Quest for Fire* and *Missing Link*. A variety of documentaries shown on public television or available for sale or rental on videocassette can also carry you to the depths of the Atlantic Ocean, the heart of a rain forest, or the inside of an urban housing project.

On Day 21, therefore, we'd like you to spend several hours watching feature films, documentaries, or even TV sitcoms related, in some fashion, to your chosen subject. These films can be anything you deem appropriate—from such phenomenal documentaries as *Shoah, Memory of the Camps*, and *The Fatal Attraction of Adolf Hitler* to witness the criminal abuses of the Third Reich, for example, to such ill-conceived and tasteless shows as "Hogan's Heroes," the charming television sitcom about the joys of concentration camp living with those fun-loving Nazis. If at all possible, in fact, the selections you choose for today's viewing should cover widely diverging points of view. You might choose a work of historical fiction, for example, followed by a comedy treatment of your field, followed by a straightforward documentary feature.

Your goal is not only to immerse yourself in your chosen subject from a variety of celluloid perspectives; it is also to observe and experience the prevailing propaganda surrounding your particular field to whatever extent may be possible.

Hemispheric Hint—Even if you think there may be no film treatments of your field, believe us, there are. Remember, you need not be literal in your selections. Ask your local video store employee for help.

After you have watched at least three or four different types of feature films and documentaries dealing with your chosen subject—and possibly eaten enough popcorn to initiate a short-term shutdown of your intestines—you should take a break of at least an hour before proceeding to the next phase of today's session.

For the second phase of today's exercise, retire to your right-brain refuge and enter a state of alert relaxation.

Hemispheric Hint—You may achieve this altered state with the help of your "Under the Volcano" tape, or simply by visualizing currents of mental energy progressively warming and relaxing your muscles.

After you have entered the state of alert relaxation, allow any lingering images from your personal film festival to spontaneously emerge in your imagination. Then imagine how you would feel if you were a character in one of the feature films or documentaries you watched earlier. Allow yourself to experience this fantasy on as personal a level as possible—how would you react in the heat of battle during the Allied invasion at Normandy, for example, or standing up at bat in the last inning of the final game of the World Series, with the score tied, two men out, and the bases loaded? How would you have felt if you were the Egyptian Queen Cleopatra or the visionary Joan of Arc?

After you have allowed yourself to experience your fantasy for twenty to thirty minutes, you will shift your focus and consider the similarities between your own everyday experience and reality as expressed in the films. If you were watching a collection of films about the Civil War, for example, you may find yourself struck by the realization that we have not progressed very far in relations between the races since that bloody chapter in human history. If you were watching films about life on the bottom of the ocean, you may find yourself considering your own role in the global ecology and the ways in which your life is influenced by what happens deep under water. Whatever your particular subject, you may also feel yourself becoming more aware of the ways in which your own attitudes and opinions are influenced by the prevailing propaganda surrounding your chosen field. You may also find yourself considering the ways in which this propaganda has influenced attitudes toward your field in the culture at large.

Now it's time to conclude today's session. Open your eyes, wiggle your fingers and toes, and return to a state of ordinary waking consciousness.

Hemispheric Hint—Continue to incubate lucid and nonlucid dreams on your field of interest and to practice dream-recollection techniques upon waking up in the morning.

Congratulations! You have just completed Week Three of the Whole Mind Program. We suggest that you celebrate by turning off your TV and VCR for a while and talking to a friend.

WEEK THREE THE YIN AND YANG OF LEARNING

DAY 15
LUCID-DREAM
LEARNING

Continue with the reality checks introduced on Day 14.

Spend some time letting your thoughts roam freely over your creative or intellectual pursuits. Tell yourself that you will come to a new, deeper, and more profound understanding of the subject matter in your dreams.

About an hour before you plan to go to bed, gather a few objects that symbolize some significant aspects of your chosen field. Place these objects near your bedside and casually contemplate their symbolic

significance to your subject.

Get in bed and write an incubation phrase that expresses some overall concern about your chosen subject. Then turn out the lights, relax, and allow yourself to drift off to sleep.

Focus on entering a lucid-dream state, just as you did on Day 14, with the tag phrase *The next time I have a dream, I will recognize that I am dreaming.*

As you drift off to sleep, focus your thoughts on the most fascinating aspects of your subject and on your need to gain

insight into your field. Don't focus so intensely on any of these ideas that you'll keep yourself awake.

If you wake up from a nonlucid dream in the middle of the night, remember to play back the dream in your mind. This time, add two details: some aspect of your chosen subject and the image of yourself being conscious of the dream as it occurs.

If you find yourself having a lucid dream that deals directly with your concerns, use it to explore your own inner relationship to your

subject and to resolve any creative or conceptual roadblocks you might have.

Practice dream-recollection techniques upon waking up and write down any impressions of your remembered dreams.

Carefully evaluate any creative ideas or images that emerge from incubated dreams from the perspective of rational, waking consciousness.

DAY 16 TUNNELING	**DAY 17** RIGHT-BRAIN WRITING		**DAY 18** READING FOR POETS
Enter a state of alert relaxation in your right-brain refuge. Visualize yourself effectively studying. Study your chosen subject at the time and place you imagined during your visualization experience.	Gather a blank piece of paper, a pen or pencil, and at least half a dozen different-colored felt-tip pens. Write the name of your topic in the middle of the paper, then draw a circle around what you've written. Begin the clustering technique by allowing your thoughts to roam freely. Jot down any ideas and associations that come to mind. You may also draw quick and simple pictures to symbolize your concepts. Place these words and pictures anywhere on the page that feels appropriate, circling them as	you go along, and making no deliberate effort to organize them. When you run out of words and pictures, use the colored pens to draw lines between the various circled words, connecting concepts that belong together in the same colors, and allowing patterns to emerge. Study your chosen subject for at least an hour.	Take the text or texts with which you are working and flip through them randomly. Look at the various chapter headings and notice whether any patterns emerge that catch your interest. Pay particular attention to any pictures, charts, or graphs that explain the topic as a whole. As soon as your interest in one area flags, go on to the next. After the 30-minute right-brain reading session, take out the clustering tools you used yesterday and create a cluster based on your experience. *(continued)*

WEEK THREE THE YIN AND YANG OF LEARNING
(continued)

DAY 18 READING THE POETS	DAY 19 MIXED METAPHORS		DAY 20 SEEING THE ELEPHANT
After you have created this cluster, contemplate the ways in which it relates to the patterns within your book or books.

If reading is not one of the tools you use to study your subject, spend the day immersed in your topic on whatever level you choose. Then spend 20 to 30 minutes organizing the day's activities in your mind through clustering. | Spend 30 to 60 minutes engaged in your chosen topic.

Go to your right-brain refuge and enter a state of alert relaxation. As you feel yourself becoming more relaxed, allow images associated with your chosen field to flow through your imagination. As you notice these images passing through your mind, search for metaphors with which to define your topic.

Once you have arrived at a suitable metaphor, return to a normal state of waking awareness. | Take a break. Then spend at least an hour playfully exploring the metaphor. | Choose an accessible real-life setting that will immerse you in your chosen field on as many sensory levels as possible.

Explore your surroundings for at least an hour.

Sit quietly in a stimulating spot in your field trip location.

Observe your surroundings.

Relax, take a deep breath, and listen to the sound of your breathing. Gradually expand your focus of attention to include the other sounds around you in your immediate environment. |

Move around your immediate environment on foot and, as you do so, pay attention to the layers of sound that surround you. Note how certain sounds draw your immediate attention while others seem to fade into the background. Spend a minimum of 15 minutes practicing this sensory focusing exercise with your sens of hearing as your guide.

Return to the spot where you began focusing on your hearing, take a deep breath, and relax.

Concentrate on any information coming to you through

your sense of smell, focusing first on your own body and then turning your attention toward your immediate environment.

Begin moving around your environment. As you do so, continue to focus on the variety of smells around you. Spend a minimum of 15 minutes focusing on your sense of smell.

Take a 15- to 20-minute break.

Once again, relax in the field trip location you have chosen. Take a deep breath and slowly let it out. Then close your eyes and imagine that you are at

the center of activity in the location you have chosen. Continue the combined visualization and sensory awareness phase of this exercise for at least another 15 or 20 minutes.

Spend another hour exploring your field trip surroundings in any manner you find appropriate.

WEEK THREE THE YIN AND YANG
OF LEARNING (continued)

DAY 21
MOTIF OF
THE MOVING
IMAGE

Spend several hours watching feature films, documentaries, or even TV sitcoms related, in some fashion, to your chosen subject.

Go to your right-brain refuge and enter a state of alert relaxation. Allow images from your personal film festival to spontaneously emerge in your imagination.

Imagine how you would feel if you were a character in one of the feature films or documentaries you watched earlier.

Experience your fantasy for 20 to 30 minutes. Then shift your focus and consider the similarities between your own everyday experience and reality as expressed in the films.

Consider the ways in which your attitudes have been influenced by the prevailing propaganda of your chosen field.

Return to a state of ordinary waking consciousness.

WEEK FOUR

SOARING TO THE ZEN STATE

WEEK FOUR

•

SOARING TO THE ZEN STATE

At its most effective, learning is an organic, poetic, natural activity in which you are totally and joyously immersed. To understand your subject on its deepest level, you must virtually be one with it—you must live it and breathe it and feel it in your bones, at least for part of the day. Achieving this state of complete focus during the learning process requires a spontaneous, intuitive involvement—in short, a state of mind most researchers now associate with the right brain. When you've achieved this state—called the "flow state"—time passes quickly and your mind zips along, grasping patterns and concepts with ease. You are *in the zone*.

To many, this perfect, fluid realm is much like the Zen state, in which self-centeredness fades and the activity of the moment fills your conscious awareness. In Week Four of the Whole Mind Program we will take you to the pinnacle of right-brain learning as you enter the Zen state and experience flow.

In a couple of potent exercises, for instance, you will learn to induce intense waking fantasies similar to those reportedly induced by the Dream Yogis of ancient Tibet. These extremely vivid visualizations should take you closer to the core of your topic than you have ever been before.

Week Four exercises will also help you learn the skill of "mindfulness," the ability to eliminate distractions and stay deeply involved in every aspect of the learning experience from one second to the next. In an exercise called "Lost in the Snow Dome," for instance, you will learn to empty your conscious mind of all interfering thoughts. In another exercise, called "The Zen Shower," you will focus on every detail of your morning shower, then adapt the focusing technique to help you master ecology, say, or math. After you have mastered these focusing techniques, Week Four exercises will help you stay in the zone—first for an hour and then for hours at a time. After you have truly mastered the Week Four exercises, you should be able to enter and maintain the flow state and call upon the powers of the right brain at will.

DAY 22

INSTANT KARMA

Entering the state of alert relaxation is an excellent way to prime your right brain for absorbing the subject matter of your field. But as you continue to pursue your subject, you may want to enter and leave this altered state of consciousness more quickly. One way of accomplishing this is to invoke a mantra, a key word that automatically helps you reach this heightened state without the need to progressively relax your muscles or visit your right-brain refuge.

To find your personal mantra, first enter a state of alert relaxation either with the help of your "Under the Volcano" tape or by visualizing each muscle relaxing in turn. After you have entered an alert-relaxed state, search through your memories for the most calming personal image you can remember. Images that people have chosen include picnicking by a lake, sitting by a fireplace in a comfortable chair and reading a book, and fishing in a river. Take time to consider this carefully and choose an image that has unique personal meaning for you. Once you arrive at this image, a close friend, fellow student, mentor, or coach should ask you questions that will assist you in rendering it as vividly as possible in your mind. For instance, if you have chosen a picnic by a lake, the friend should ask such questions as "Is the sun shining brightly? What kind of food are you eating? Who's with you? Are you sitting or reclining on the grass?" After you have answered these questions, imagine the scene as vividly as you can.

Now select a cue word to represent the scene you have envisioned. For instance, if you best achieve alert relaxation by picturing a picnic at a lake, your cue word might be *lake, water*, or even something as far afield as *hot dog*. Repeat the word and let the image become fully associated in your thoughts with the state of alert relaxation that you are now experiencing. By doing so, you should learn to enter an alert-relaxed state more efficiently in the future simply by repeating this cue word, or mantra, in your thoughts.

Spend as much of the rest of the day as possible immersed in your topic. Every time your focus seems to drift, concentrate on your mantra. Give yourself a minute or two to return—more fully alert and more deeply relaxed—to your intuitive, spontaneous self.

Finally, choose a one-hour period this evening during which you will be completely undisturbed and enter your right-brain refuge. Enter a state of alert relaxation. When you have achieved it, open your eyes and begin to study, review, visualize, or otherwise engage in your particular learning activity. Allow yourself to feel as close to your topic as possible. Feel in sync with its rhythms and in tune with its subtle movements. Every time your mind starts to drift, even for a moment, focus on your mantra and let go of the interfering thought. Leave as little emotional and intellectual distance between your mind and the topic of study as possible.

Hemispheric Hint—Remember to induce lucid and nonlucid dreams on your topic of interest and to practice dream-recollection techniques upon awakening.

Hemispheric Hint—Continue to reinforce the altered state of alert relaxation throughout the learning process with the help of your mantra.

DAY 23

THE ZEN SHOWER

Today you'll practice yet another technique for achieving total focus. Suggested by J. J. Gibbs, author of *Dancing with Your Books: The Zen Way of Studying*, "The Zen Shower" teaches you to focus totally on the act of taking a shower. After you have learned to focus on your shower, you should be able to use similar techniques to focus on the topic at hand.

To begin the exercise simply retire to your bathroom, get undressed, and get into the shower. As you shower, think of nothing but the shower itself. Pay attention to every detail of your shower experience moment by moment.

Gibbs describes the experience this way: "When I wash my face, I become conscious of each part of it. I'm aware of my eyes, then my nose, then my mouth, as my soapy hands glide over them. I feel the individual streams of water as they rinse the soap from my face.

"As I wash, I become washing. There is no 'I' doing the washing. There is no washing being done. There is only the activity of washing in which the water, soap, and man become one. When thoughts of 'I' doing the washing enter my mind, I let them go. When thoughts of doing something other than showering pop into consciousness, I do not cling to them. I stay centered in the activity of the moment—showering."

Spend from twenty to forty minutes taking the kind of shower described above. Focus completely and exclusively on the experience of the shower, pushing all other thoughts and distractions out of your mind.

When you have completed your shower, go out and appreciate the best that mundane reality has to offer. But instead of just eating breakfast, say, or taking a walk, focus on every moment and every rich detail of your everyday life just as you focused on your shower.

When you feel ready, return to your right-brain refuge and once again immerse yourself in your subject. Stay with it from moment to moment in every detail, just as you stayed with your shower earlier in the day.

Hemispheric Hint—From now on, take a Zen shower every morning after you wake up. Focus on every detail of your shower, and pay attention to nothing else. After a bit of practice, you should be able to bring the same minute focus, the same flow state, to all that you do.

Hemispheric Hint—Remember to induce lucid and nonlucid dreams on your topic of interest, to practice dream-recollection techniques upon awakening, and to record your dreams in your dream diary.

Hemispheric Hint—Continue to reinforce the alert-relaxation state throughout the learning process with the help of your mantra.

Hemispheric Hint—Practice controlled dreaming at some point during today's study session for an especially potent experience in right-brain learning.

DAY 24

LOST IN THE
SNOW DOME

One of the most important tools for effective right-brain learning—and learning in general—is emptying your mind of all distractions so that you can focus on the topic at hand. To help you achieve this focus, therefore, we present a technique to help you whenever your mind wanders and whenever you find it difficult to focus on your work. In essence, today's exercise will help you empty your mind of virtually all thoughts. You may then fill up this tabula rasa however you wish.

Hemispheric Hint—Read the rest of the instructions for Day 24 before sitting down to do the exercise.

Begin by practicing a deep and measured form of breathing often called "centered breathing." To do so, lie down on a carpeted or padded portion of your floor and close your eyes. Enter a state of alert relaxation. Then take a series of deep breaths from your diaphragm. Slowly breathe in and out through your mouth for five to ten minutes.

After you have become extremely relaxed, sit with your spine erect and continue to focus on your breathing. Feel the continuous presence of your breath as it rises and falls against your abdominal wall and moves millimeter by millimeter through your entire body. Breathe in as quietly and slowly as possible, so that if somebody placed a tiny thread in front of your nose, it wouldn't budge. Exhale even more slowly. Leave a tiny pause (or even hold your breath for a moment) between each inhalation and exhalation. This fixation on your breath will help prevent intrusive thoughts. Inevitably some feelings, impressions, or physical sensations will invade, but let them float away in the movement and rhythm of your breathing.

Hemispheric Hint—Do not hyperventilate. Also be cautious about this exercise if you suffer from emphysema, heart trouble, or similar conditions. Finally, if you are on antipsychotic drugs, please refrain from this exercise.

Now close your eyes and focus on the sensation of purity and emptiness. You may focus on breathing itself. If you would like a visual image to help you capture the sensation of emptiness, you may envision an unblemished snow field or an endless screen of soft white light. You may also imagine yourself inside a large, glass-encased, water-filled snow dome (the sort of thing that often comes with a Statue of Liberty inside) with torrents of gentle snow falling all around. Let the emptiness wash over you for several minutes, clearing your mind.

Once your mind is completely empty and cleared of all distractions, you may proceed with your learning efforts. Spend the next two hours as deeply immersed in your topic as possible. Whenever your mind begins to wander, focus on your breathing and call up the image of a snow field, a snow dome, or an endless screen of soft white light. Use the soothing mental image to help clear your mind and to help you focus your thoughts, once more, on your chosen subject.

> **Hemispheric Hint**—You may modify the "Lost in the Snow Dome" exercise to complement many of the exercises in this book. Whenever maintaining a steady focus becomes a problem, this technique should help you work it through.

> **Hemispheric Hint**—Once you have mastered "Lost in the Snow Dome," you may use the technique whenever you feel distracted.

> **Hemispheric Hint**—Practice controlled dreaming at some point during today's study session for an especially potent experience in right-brain learning.

DAY 25

TIBETAN TRUTHS

Using a potent method of guided imagery, the Dream Yogis of ancient Tibet are said to have withdrawn more and more deeply inside themselves until they began to dream. But these dreams were different from ordinary dreams, because the yogis never truly fell asleep; in fact, they never even completely lost conscious awareness.

The exercise below will enable you to tap the Dream Yogis' approach through a more modern, less difficult, technique referred to as "controlled dreaming." In essence, controlled dreaming is a more advanced, more intense, and more potent form of alert relaxation. While immersed in a controlled dream, you should find your ability to visualize—and thus absorb—your topic drastically increased.

According to University of Colorado psychologist Richard Suinn, who developed a form of controlled dreaming to help train athletes and others, the technique may represent a new form of learning. Suinn finds the technique especially helpful to those who must master the skills for performance, be it Alpine skiing or public speaking. "When we enter this uncharted realm," Suinn suggests, "we might be creating a template—a baseline model for performance—that would guide the physical and mental processes that occur during the actual event." Controlled dreaming, adds Suinn, should enable you to tap the visualization of the dream state while awake. Suinn's specific technique, called visuo-motor behavior rehearsal, or VMBR, has proven so successful with athletes that some sports psychologists say that the participants' brain waves and muscle patterns, as measured by electrodes, mimic patterns exhibited during participation in the actual sports events themselves.

As far as we are concerned, controlled dreaming can be an important part of the learning arsenal for virtually any skill or topic. As you go over the details of your subject in this enhanced state of alert relaxation, these details should become part of your overall gestalt. They should therefore become embedded not just in your brain, but in your body as well.

Begin the "Tibetan Truths" exercise by going into your right-brain refuge and entering the state of alert relaxation. Then, think about your long-range learning goals, as well as your specific learning goals for today's session. You should also take notes on these goals to help focus your thoughts.

> **Hemispheric Hint**—You may write in a conventional fashion or, if you prefer, you may utilize the clustering technique you learned during Week Three.

As you write, ask yourself what it is that you want to learn, be it novel writing, skiing, or organic chemistry. Let's say your overall goal is studying evolution and your goal for today is going over the chemical evolution of the first organic molecules on earth.

Once you have set your goal, spend at least an hour studying with today's specific learning mission in mind. Tapping any helpful right-brain learning techniques presented throughout the days and weeks of the Whole Mind Program, read about and study chemical evolution as potently as you possibly can.

After you have immersed yourself in your field for an hour, continue to maintain the state of alert relaxation. If you find it difficult, use your "Under the Volcano" tape.

Because the controlled-dreaming technique is so intense, you should now deepen your state of alert relaxation through centered breathing. The technique is particularly important for control because, according to sports psychologists who frequently use centered breathing with clients, it seems to change your body's center of gravity, increasing the feeling of internal stability and enhancing your ability to focus. To practice centered breathing, lie down on a carpeted or padded portion of your floor and close your eyes. Then take a series of deep breaths from your diaphragm. Slowly breathe in and out through your mouth for five to ten minutes.

If you have followed our instructions closely, your left brain has been tuned down and your right brain has intensified its focus. You should therefore be primed to enter the deepened state of controlled dreaming. To do so, simply close your eyes and immerse yourself in mental images of the task or subject you wish to master. If you wish to understand chemical evolution as intuitively and deeply as possible, for example, imagine life's first tiny molecules spinning and swirling through the primordial sea. Envision the early sunlight and water impacting on the molecules and see, as vividly as possible in your mind's eye, the precursors of life emerging.

As you visualize, return, in your mind's eye, to the material you absorbed in the first part of this exercise, playing it over in your imagination until it takes on its own vital, natural organization, fitting, like a long-treasured memory, into the shape of your innermost patterns and thoughts. If chemical evolution is your topic, experience, as completely and graphically as possible, the three-dimensional shapes and movements of organic molecules as they merge to form life.

Do not crowd this visualization exercise with external phrases or thoughts, such as, "I really am very relaxed," or "I'm getting this subject in a whole new way." Instead, stay with your topic and your goal; stay on the path. Experience yourself as one with your topic, and treat the images you are spinning as essential counterpoints to your own existence. As new and surprising images emerge, you should find yourself approaching your topic with a new and surprising sense of harmony, direction, and flow.

Hemispheric Hint—Remember to practice controlled dreaming once a day for the duration of the Whole Mind Program.

Hemispheric Hint—Remember to induce lucid and nonlucid dreams on your topic of interest and to practice dream-recollection techniques, and to record your dreams in your dream diary upon awakening.

Hemispheric Hint—Continue to reinforce the state of alert relaxation throughout the learning process with the help of your mantra.

DAY 26

HIGH LUCID
LEARNING

      On Day 26 you will combine the controlled-dreaming method you learned on Day 25 with the dream incubation and lucid dreaming techniques you've been practicing throughout the Whole Mind Program.

      To practice today's exercise, continue the daily reality checks you've been using to encourage lucid dreaming. Also, continue to gently remind yourself of your openness to lucid dreams. Then, spend at least an hour just before bedtime studying some aspect of your chosen subject. When you have completed this study session, make a cluster to express your current thinking on your overall field of interest; make sure to include in this cluster the relationship between the overall topic and the subtopic that you focused on today.

      After you have made this cluster, get ready for bed. Then, just before you turn off the light and go to sleep, take your dream diary and write a phrase that expresses a question about your chosen topic. Finally, as you're falling asleep, use the controlled-dreaming technique you practiced in yesterday's session as an especially focused form of dream incubation.

      Lie on your back in bed with your eyes closed and focus on the sounds and feelings associated with your breathing. As you do so, enter a state of alert relaxation. As you become more relaxed, allow your mind to fill with images relating to your field of interest. As these images become more intense, imagine them surrounding you in three dimensions. Continue to focus on the images, and on the sounds and feelings you associate with breathing; at the same time, allow yourself to become so deeply relaxed that you finally drift off into sleep and dreaming.

Using this approach, it is quite likely that you will find yourself dreaming—if not lucid dreaming—about your chosen field. With practice, you may even find yourself moving directly into a lucid dream with little or no sense of having lost conscious awareness prior to the lucid dream.

Whether or not this happens for you the first time you try this, you may still use the approach of ''falling backward'' into a lucid or nonlucid dream, combined with the controlled-dreaming approach, upon first awakening. As soon as you feel yourself waking up, either the first thing in the morning or sometime during the night, focus on images relating to your chosen field just as you did while falling asleep. Then, without opening your eyes or even moving, allow yourself to fall back asleep—and back into your dreams—while immersed in mental images relating to your field.

Hemispheric Hint—Remember to apply the dream-recollection techniques, and to record all your dreams in your dream diary upon awakening.

Hemispheric Hint—Although much of the Whole Mind Program makes use of dream incubation and other techniques designed to help you exert a more conscious influence over the course and subject matter of your dreams, we do not recommend that you practice such techniques to the exclusion of "free dreaming"—ordinary dreaming without any effort at deliberate interference. While dream incubation and lucid dreaming can be potent techniques for tapping into your right brain and heightening your general sense of self-awareness, it also seems evident that plain, old-fashioned dreaming serves its own complex psychological purposes and should therefore be given free reign to occur on its own terms as often as possible.

DAY 27

GO WITH
THE FLOW

University of Chicago psychologist Mihaly Csikszentmihalyi has described an extraordinarily focused state of consciousness he calls "the flow state," or, more simply, "flow." You may have experienced this state yourself—when you become so absorbed in a particular task, for example, that several hours pass by in what seems like less than a single hour, or when your participation in a given activity causes everything else to fade, pushing your performance far past your expectations. The flow state is considered an optimal state for learning because it enhances your ability to focus; as a bonus, the flow state boosts your ability to mentally organize the information at hand.

You may have found yourself entering the flow state spontaneously while practicing many of the exercises in the Whole Mind Program. On Day 27, however, you will learn techniques for entering this exceptionally focused state at will.

Hemispheric Hint—Because today's exercise requires some preparation, read through the instructions that follow before carrying them out.

Begin by selecting a piece of instrumental music that builds gently and gradually from a few basic instruments playing in subtle harmony into a powerfully organized crescendo involving an entire orchestra. An excellent example of such a composition is Pachelbel's Canon in D Major. According to Csikszentmihalyi, in his highly recommended book, *Flow: The Psychology of Optimal Experience*, "Music, which is organized auditory information, helps organize the mind that attends to it, and therefore reduces psychic entropy, or the disorder we experience when random information interferes with goals. Listening to music wards off boredom and anxiety, and when seriously attended to, it can induce flow experiences." The key here is not merely playing the music in the background, but actively listening to the music so that it can affect your mental state on a deep, inner level.

Once you have selected an appropriate piece of music, you'll need to make one more special arrangement. Prepare an extra-long audio-cassette to include an initial twenty minutes of blank tape and then the musical selection you have chosen, in full, on the remaining portion of the same side of the tape. (If you are fortunate enough to have the use of an auto-reverse cassette recorder, which automatically plays both sides of the tape, you can simply leave one side entirely blank and record your musical selection on the other.)

Once you have made these essential preparations, set up your tape player in a convenient spot in your right-brain refuge. Before you enter your right-brain refuge to begin the exercise, take a Zen shower just as you did on Day 23. Then, as soon as the shower is finished, retire immediately to your right-brain refuge. (You may wish to wear a comfortable bathrobe for the occasion, so that you won't become distracted by fiddling around with your clothes.) Relax in a comfortable spot and switch on the tape player so that the blank part of the tape begins cycling through the machine. Focus on your breathing and enter a state of alert relaxation. As you become more deeply relaxed, envision yourself attaining complete mastery of your chosen field. Then, gradually, let these images fade into the void and allow your mind to become blank.

Continue to passively enjoy the serene sensations associated with your alert-relaxed state until you begin to hear the music playing in the background. As you listen to the music, notice any emotions or physical sensations that it may stir. Experience the music as though it were emerging from the deepest part of your being.

As you listen to the music, notice it building toward its conclusion. As the music ends, consciously direct your focus toward the learning task you have chosen and gradually bring yourself out of your alert-relaxed state. Allow yourself to experience a sense of confidence and personal power as you return to full waking awareness and turn your attention toward the task at hand.

With practice, and perhaps even the first time you try this, you should find yourself entering the intensely focused mental state known as "flow." At this point, simply become completely absorbed in your learning process. Whenever you want, you may also return to a more intense focus by once again playing your musical flow selection and taking some time to fully appreciate and listen to the music.

DAY 28

IN THE ZONE

The flow state can become a vital component of right-brain learning; as such, it is well worth the exclusive focus of a second day, especially as you move toward graduation from the Whole Mind Program. On Day 28, therefore, simply repeat the exercise of Day 27 with a small variation: For today's flow exercise, choose an entire album that can help you maintain the desired focus. (Many of the Windham Hill recordings are suitable for this purpose. We especially recommend George Winston's *Autumn* and *Winter Into Spring*. We also recommend *Petals,* released by Rising Sun Records in Mill Valley, California. Some people we know have been quite successful at achieving flow with rock music. Some excellent albums for this purpose include U2's *Joshua Tree, The John Lennon Collection*, and Roy Orbison's *In Dreams*. We have written entire books while listening to these albums.) Of course, music appreciation is a matter of personal taste (or the lack of it), so we recommend that you choose a kind of music that you find has the desired effect for you.

Once you have chosen such an album (or albums), proceed with the rest of this exercise just as you did in yesterday's session. Then, as you move directly into the studying phase of today's session, replace the flow tape in your tape player with one of the long-playing albums you've selected. Alternatively, you may play the album on a CD player or stereo, if you have either of these systems available. The key to this exercise is having the music recycling in the background for several hours, creating an undercurrent of rhythm and focus that will help you to organize your thought patterns and maintain a state of flow throughout the course of a lengthy study session. You may drive your roommates, spouse, or neighbors crazy in the process, but you may also find yourself amazed at how much learning takes place.

Hemispheric Hint—To avoid disturbing anyone around you, you may find it worthwhile to invest in a set of stereo headphones, especially if you plan to use this highly effective approach to learning regularly.

Congratulations! You've just completed Week Four of the Whole Mind Program.

WEEK FOUR SOARING TO THE ZEN STATE

DAY 22 INSTANT KARMA		DAY 23 THE ZEN SHOWER	
Enter a state of alert relaxation. Search through your memories for the most calming personal image you can remember. Have a friend ask you questions about this image. Select a key word, or mantra, to represent the scene you have envisioned. Repeat the word and let the image become fully associated in your thoughts with the state of alert relaxation that you are now experiencing. Spend as much of the rest of the day as possible immersed in your topic. Every time	your focus seems to drift, concentrate on your mantra. Choose a one-hour period to study, and as you do so, maintain your focus with the help of your mantra.	Retire to your bathroom, get undressed, and get into the shower. As you shower for 20 to 40 minutes, think of nothing but the shower itself. When you have completed your shower, go out and appreciate the best that mundane reality has to offer. But instead of just eating breakfast, say, or taking a walk, focus on every moment and every rich detail of your everyday life just as you focused on your shower. When you feel ready, return to your right-brain refuge and once again immerse yourself in your	subject. Stay with it from moment to moment in every detail, just as you stayed with your shower earlier in the day.

DAY 24 LOST IN THE SNOW DOME	DAY 25 TIBETAN TRUTHS	DAY 26 HIGH LUCID LEARNING	
Practice centered breathing.

Focus on the act of centered breathing.

Close your eyes and focus on the sensation of purity and emptiness. If you want, invoke the image of a blank screen, snow field, or snow dome.

Once your mind is completely empty and cleared of all distractions, you may proceed with your learning efforts. Spend the next two hours deeply immersed in your topic. Whenever your mind begins to wander, focus on your breathing and call up the appropriate image. | Enter your right-brain refuge and enter the state of alert relaxation. Think about and take notes on your learning goals.

Spend at least an hour studying.

Deepen your alert-relaxed state through centered breathing.

Close your eyes and immerse yourself in vivid mental images of the task or subject you wish to master. | Continue the daily "reality checks" you've been using to encourage lucid dreaming. Also continue to gently remind yourself of your openness to lucid dreams.

Spend at least an hour just before bedtime studying some aspect of your chosen subject.

Make a cluster to express your current thinking on your overall field of interest.

Get ready for bed.

Take your dream diary and write a phrase that expresses a question about your chosen topic. | As you're falling asleep, lie on your back in bed with your eyes closed and focus on the sounds and feelings associated with your breathing. As you do so, enter a state of alert relaxation. As you become more relaxed, allow your mind to fill with images relating to your field of interest.

Drift off into sleep and dreaming. |

WEEK FOUR SOARING TO THE ZEN STATE (continued)

DAY 27 GO WITH THE FLOW			DAY 28 IN THE ZONE

Select a piece of instrumental music that builds gently and gradually from a few basic instruments playing in subtle harmony into a powerfully organized crescendo involving an entire orchestra.

Prepare an extra-long audio cassette to include an initial 20 minutes of blank tape and then the musical selection you have chosen, in full, on the remaining portion of the same side of the tape.

Set up your tape player in a convenient spot in your right-brain refuge.

Take a Zen shower.

Go to your right-brain refuge, relax in a comfortable spot, and switch on the tape player so that the blank part of the tape begins cycling through the machine.

Focus on your breathing and enter a state of alert relaxation.

Envision yourself attaining complete mastery of your chosen field.

Allow your mind to become blank.

Continue to passively enjoy the serene sensations associated with your alert-relaxed state until you begin to hear

the music playing in the background. As you listen to the music, notice any emotions or physical sensations that it may stir. Experience the music as though it were emerging from the deepest part of your being.

As you listen to the music, notice it building toward its end. As the music concludes, consciously direct your focus toward the learning task you have chosen and gradually bring yourself out of your alert-relaxed state.

Turn your attention toward the task at hand.

Select a long-playing album that builds to a powerfully organized crescendo.

Set up your tape player in a convenient spot in your right-brain refuge.

Take a Zen shower.

Go to your right-brain refuge, relax in a comfortable spot, and play the flow tape you created on Day 27.

Focus on your breathing and enter a state of alert relaxation.

Envision yourself attaining complete mastery of your chosen field.

Allow your mind to become blank.

Continue to passively enjoy the serene sensations associated with your alert-relaxed state until you begin to hear the music playing in the background. As you listen to the music, notice any emotions or physical sensations that it may stir. Experience the music as though it were emerging from the deepest part of your being.

As you listen to the music, notice it building toward its end. As the music concludes, consciously direct your focus toward the learning task you have chosen and gradually bring yourself out of your alert-relaxed state.

Turn your attention toward the task at hand. Play your long-playing album as you become completely absorbed in your learning process.

DAYS 29 AND 30

CREATING A
RIGHT-BRAIN
PROGRAM OF
YOUR OWN

At its most powerful and effective, of course, right-brain learning is not merely a 30-day program of mental exercises but a long-term, perhaps even lifelong, process. Many of the techniques you have been practicing in the Whole Mind Program, in fact, will prove most beneficial if you continue to practice them regularly, applying them to learning your chosen subject in a customized manner suited to the demands of your particular field, as well as to your personal preferences.

Days 29 and 30 of the Whole Mind Program should therefore be spent totally immersed in learning about your chosen field and creating a right-brain learning program of your own. Begin by reviewing the various headings listed in the table of contents at the beginning of this book. (If you have any trouble recalling all the details of a particular exercise, simply refer directly to the printed text.) As you review these headings, make a special note of those techniques you feel are most appropriate for learning about your particular topic. Then turn to the corresponding pages in the text and mark these with paper clips so that you can locate them easily in the future.

If you are studying the anthropological background of the Haida culture of the Northwest coast of North America, for example, you might select a multisensory exercise involving various tribal artifacts and tribal music, if these are available to you, along with a guided imagery and visualization exercise in which you imagine yourself as a mask being used in a tribal ceremony. You might also create an inner mentor exercise involving a native shaman and a fantasia exercise in which you envision yourself as a totem pole overlooking a tribal village. Of course, you will also want to include in your personal program the more basic techniques of alert relaxation, clustering, dream work, and flow states.

As you continue to practice these techniques and apply them to study in your chosen field, you should also continue to fully utilize any traditional left-brain learning approaches that have worked for you in the past. Right-brain learning, as many leading educators have pointed out, is most effective as part of a holistic learning process involving both linear and nonlinear modes of thought.

We hope you have enjoyed and benefited from your participation in the Whole Mind Program and wish you all the best in your future learning experiences. We also extend our warmest wishes and con- gratulations. You've just graduated from the Whole Mind Program!

APPENDIX A
A SPECIAL NOTE TO THE PHYSICALLY DISABLED

*F*or the sake of simplicity, the instructions for many of the exercises in the Whole Mind Program appear to assume certain basic physical capabilities. We sincerely hope, however, that the Whole Mind Program will attract a diverse readership, including individuals who may have physical disabilities. In fact, there is absolutely no reason why the techniques presented in the Whole Mind Program cannot be practiced by everyone.

In much of our research at the Institute for Advanced Psychology, disabled individuals have made a significant contribution to our exploration and understanding of a wide range of extended human capabilities. We therefore request that our disabled readers bear with us, and that they feel free to adapt the various Whole Mind exercises to their personal capabilities and preferences.

We suggest, for example, that if you are blind, hearing impaired, usually in a wheelchair, or otherwise restricted in your ability to easily move around your environment, you simply adjust the exercises to your particular needs; we assure you that the program will work just as well. We also remind you that many of the Whole Mind exercises are easily adaptable to a wide variety of available sensory and psychological approaches. If necessary, it is completely acceptable to skip a particular exercise, simply replacing it with another more suited to your requirements on a particular day. It is also always acceptable to proceed at a pace that feels most comfortable for you and works best in your individual situation.

We thank you for your interest and participation in the Whole Mind Program. We hope it will add a new dimension of enriching inner exploration and experience to your life.

—Keith Harary and Pamela Weintraub

APPENDIX B
FURTHER READING

Csikszentmihalyi, Mihaly, *Flow: The Psychology of Optimal Experience*. New York: HarperPerrenial, 1991.

Edwards, Betty, *Drawing on the Right Side of the Brain*. Los Angeles: Tarcher, 1979.

Gibbs, J. J., *Dancing With Your Books: The Zen Way of Studying*. New York: Plume, 1990.

Harary, Keith, Ph.D., and Pamela Weintraub, *Lucid Dreams in 30 Days: The Creative Sleep Program*. New York: St. Martin's Press, 1989.

Rico, Gabriele, *Writing the Natural Way*. Los Angeles: Tarcher, 1983.

Williams, Linda Verlee, *Teaching for the Two-Sided Mind: A Guide to Right Brain/Left Brain Education*. New York: Simon & Schuster, 1983.

ACKNOWLEDGMENTS

We wish to express our sincere gratitude to our spouses: Mark Teich, proof positive that the left brain is as vibrantly creative as the right, and Darlene Moore, who never ceases to teach and to learn.

We would also like to thank our colleagues and friends who have helped us gain a deeper understanding of the learning process, especially those pioneering educators and researchers whose ground-breaking work we have drawn upon in developing the Whole Mind Program. We have credited their suggestions wherever possible within the text itself. We would also like to further acknowledge that much of the Whole Mind Program would not have been possible without the invaluable contributions of the following individuals, whose insights and suggestions have been incorporated into our overall approach. Our very special appreciation to George Kokoris, Linda Verlee Williams, Gabriele Rico, Betty Edwards, Dee Williams, David Thornburg, J. J. Gibbs, Richard Suinn, Roger Sperry, and Charles Tart.

Special thanks also goes to our talented and supportive editor, Robert Weil, who came up with the 30-day concept, and Richard Romano of St. Martin's, for his additional good-natured support. We would also like to express our sincere appreciation to our literary agents, Wendy Lipkind and Roslyn Targ. Finally, thanks to *Omni* magazine, where some of the Whole Mind exercises first appeared.

We also extend our appreciation to the board of directors and board of scientific advisers of the Institute for Advanced Psychology for their role in furthering advanced psychological research.

ABOUT THE AUTHORS

Keith Harary, Ph.D., is internationally known for his pioneering contributions to scientific research on altered states of consciousness and extended human abilities. Dr. Harary, who holds a Ph.D. in psychology with emphasis in both clinical counseling and experimental psychology, has authored and co-authored more than sixty popular and professional articles on topics relating to advanced psychological research and other areas. His work has been discussed in dozens of scientific and popular publications and more than three dozen books. He is also coauthor, with Pamela Weintraub, of *Have an Out-of-Body Experience in 30 Days: The Free Flight Program; Lucid Dreams in 30 Days: The Creative Sleep Program; Mystical Experiences in 30 Days: The Higher Consciousness Program; Inner Sex in 30 Days: The Erotic Fulfillment Program; and Enhanced Memory in 30 Days: The Total-Recall Program.* He is also coauthor of the best-selling book *The Mind Race.* He is president and research director of the Institute for Advanced Psychology in San Francisco.

Pamela Weintraub is editor-at-large of *Omni* magazine, where she has worked on staff for the past ten years. She is also the author or coauthor of nine previous books, including *Nurturing the Unborn Child, You Can Save the Animals*, and *25 Things You Can Do to Beat the Recession of the 1990s.* She is coauthor, with Keith Harary, of *Have an Out-of-Body Experience in 30 Days: The Free Flight Program; Lucid Dreams in 30 Days: The Creative Sleep Program; Mystical Experiences in 30 Days: The Higher Consciousness Program; Inner Sex in 30 Days: The Erotic Fulfillment Program; and Enhanced Memory in 30 Days: The Total Recall Program.* Her articles have appeared in many national magazines from *Omni* to *Health* to *Discover*.